ARTISAN BREAD

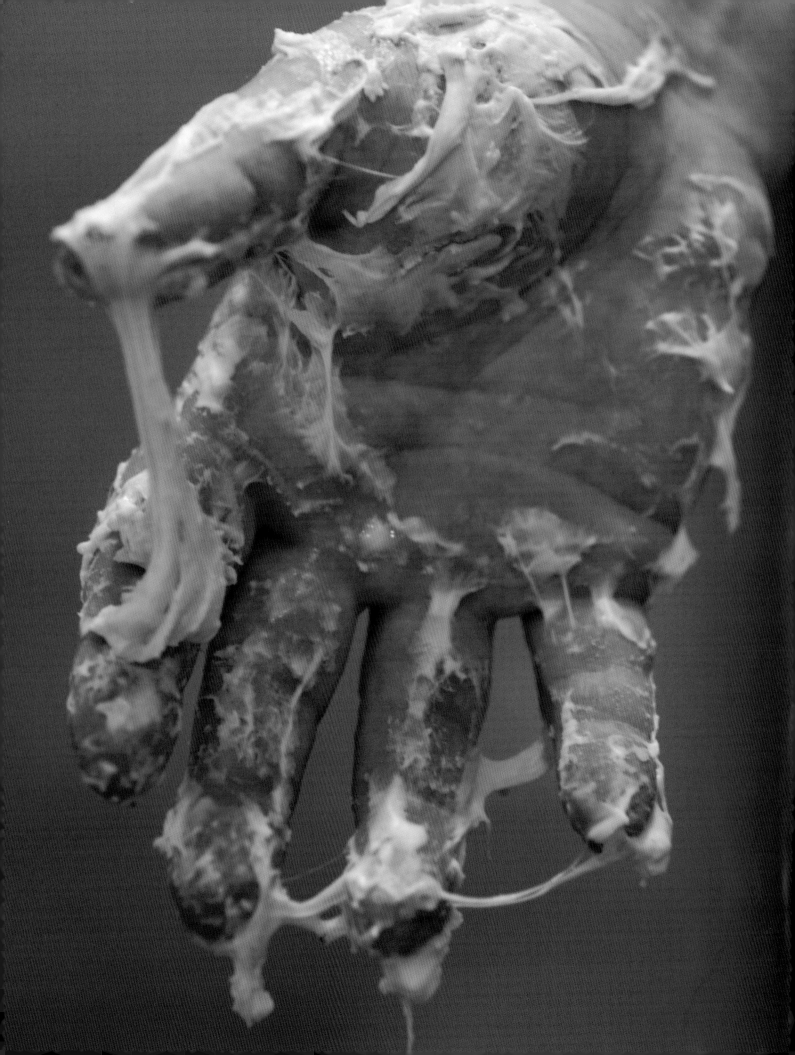

ARTISAN BREAD

Jan Hedh

Klas Andersson

© 2004 Jan Hedh and Bokförlaget Prisma, Stockholm

Originally published in Swedish as Bröd by Prisma, 2004
First published in English in 2007 by
Riverhouse West Ltd
1 Brassey Road
Old Potts Way
Shrewsbury
Shropshire SY3 7FA
England

Author: Jan Hedh
Photographs: Klas Andersson
English language translation: ©Katarina Sjöwall Trodden

Printed in Italy 2007
ISBN 978-0-9555958-0-6

Contents

Preface

There were many bakeries in the area around Bellevue-vägen in Malmö, southern Sweden, where I grew up. My mother made nearly all the bread, biscuits and cakes for the family, and I remember the lovely smell and the wonderful flavours that awaited me as I returned from school.

On special occasions we bought bread and cakes from one of the many bakeries, mainly white bread, dark rye bread and fine farmer's loaves. We bought soft breakfast rolls with flaky crusts from the patisseries. Swedberg's bakery in Malmö was famous for their plaited white bread. "Sundets bröd" was another favourite. Back then, all bread was made in bakeries, not patisseries.

Forty years ago, at the age of fourteen, I started as a pastry-cook apprentice after completing an internship at the restaurant and patisserie Residens in Malmö. I knew straight away that I wanted to be a chef or a pastry-cook. The head of the pastry department was Curt Andersson, a master craftsman who had finished off his training in Switzerland and France. He ran the patisserie with a firm hand, making sure that each cake was made properly and that the icing sparkled in the window display.

It was not until I travelled on the Continent that I learned how tasty and beautiful bread could be. When I was working at the Honold Confiserie in Zurich, I often studied the breads at the Kleiner bakery.

During my training I took a course in how to make Swiss regional breads at the Richemont school at Luzern and in regional French baking at the Lenôtre school in Paris. But it was not until the mid-1980s, when I realized how bland the bread sold in Sweden was, that I began to take a serious interest in bread.

Quality has always been important to me. If you decide to spend time doing something, it has got to be done well or you might as well not do it at all.

When I visited the United States in 2001, I noticed that many bakeries used natural sourdough and stone ovens, just like in France. This is why I got so excited when Christer Alfredsson took the initiative to open Olof Viktors at Glemminge in south-east Skåne. Today, Christer is head of Olof Viktors to ensure the continued quality of the project. (The bakery and

The industry was inundated with bread mixes, and it was the suppliers of semifinished products that steered the development of the patisserie and bakery trades. The formula was simple: just add water and yeast to the flour mix, leave the dough to prove for no more than fifteen minutes and voilà, you have a decent bread and the bakers make money ... In Sweden, this development eventually meant that there are now very few bakeries and patisseries left. In France, where they cherish quality and tradition, there are bakeries and patisseries on every street corner.

café is named after Christer's grandfather's grocery store, a really old-fashioned shop).

Robert and Linda Nilsson are part-owners. Linda has developed the sandwich concept, and together with Maria Olsson and Kajsa Nilsson I work with our breads and wide range of home-made ice creams, jams and marmalades.

At Olof Victors everything revolves around the wood-fired stone oven and the fresh, rustic breads, nearly all of them based on some form of sourdough. It is not that easy to learn to stoke and bake in a stone oven – but the quality of the bread and the crust make up for it! No other oven comes even close. Erik Olofson, a baker at the Rosendal café and shop on Djurgården in Stockholm, pioneered the use of wood-fired ovens in Sweden, and he taught us how to prepare the fire at Olof Viktors.

Many of our customers confess to being completely hooked on our bread. Apart from selling over the counter, we distribute bread to selected local shops in order to enable more people to enjoy it.

just as tasty as those you can buy at the baker's in your own home. Buy a stone slab, approximately 2 cm thick, and bake the breads straight on it. Alternatively, use a preheated baking tray. The heat will be conducted straight to the bread instead of heating up the tray.

Follow the instructions closely and always use kitchen scales rather than risk inaccuracy with a decilitre or cup measure. Also remember that flour is a perishable product that does not improve with storing.

We usually begin by making a starter on day one. On day two we knead the dough and shape the breads that are then left to rise slowly in the refrigerator until the next day when we bake them straight on the stone hearth.

I have collected some of my favourite breads in this book. Some can be purchased at Olof Viktors, others will perhaps be available sometime in the future. I hope that it will serve as inspiration for creative baking at home as well as in restaurants and bakeries. The idea is that you can make bread that is

Old, dry flour absorbs more water than fresh flour.

I am dedicating this book to my dear mother, who taught me to enjoy fresh bread and good home cooking when I was a boy.

Jan Hedh
Malmö, February 2004

INTRODUCTION

Before you Start

It is important always to use high-quality ingredients.
- Always use butter, not margarine. I recommend unsalted butter since it is fresher than salted butter.
- Always use strong flour for making basic bread. Spelt (dinkel) flour can usually be found in your local health food shop.
- Use high-quality olive oil. Virgin oil should be used for sprinkling on top of the bread, not in the dough.

Below are some tips that I have found to be very useful:
- Always use good quality digital scales that can be zeroised as you add new ingredients.
- Buy a simple steak thermometer and use it for checking the temperature of the dough and if the bread is ready.

- Weigh the ingredients on the scales and do not improvise with cup or decilitre measures.
- Follow the procedures and times strictly.
- Use an electric kitchen assistant to knead the dough. Doing it by hand is hard work and the result is never the same as with a machine since you will never have the stamina to knead it long enough to stretch the gluten properly. I have used an Electrolux and a KitchenAid stand mixer.
- Prove the bread in flour-lined baskets rather than straight on the baking tray for a higher and prettier result. Loose doughs made with less flour are supported by the basket and rise upwards. Stiff doughs can prove straight on the tray or on a towel dipped in flour. Make a crease between the breads to make them rise upwards instead of sideways for a more attractive and higher result. On the Continent bakers usually prove the dough on a towel or on a plank and not on the tray.

The professionals use different size baskets depending on the amount of dough. They come in sizes for 250 g, 500 g, 750 g and 1,000 g. There are baskets for 1,500 g, 2,000 g and up to 4,000 g for huge breads. Naturally, you can buy inexpensive proving baskets. If you want the professional version, by them in a cordon bleu shop or on the Internet.

I have tested the recipes in a stone oven as well as an ordinary kitchen oven to determine the correct baking times.

A Background to Bakers and Bakeries

The history of bread

Bread-making goes way back to prehistoric times and is known in many cultures. Ovens may have been used for making bread for the past six thousand years, and the Egyptians had bakeries 3000 B.C. A temple bakery where bread for ritual sacrifice was made 3,000 years ago has been found by the Euphrates, near Baghdad. This means that baking is a five thousand-year-old practice.

The Egyptians loved bread, and they ate about five hundred grams a day. We know that there were over thirty different kinds of bread in all shapes and sizes. Some were made especially to be put in the graves, and decorative breads were sacrificed to the gods. A wall painting with bakers has been found at the 1100 B.C. burial site of Ramses III.

The ancient Greeks too made different kinds of bread. The Romans started somewhat later, but as the Roman Empire spread eastwards, these skills were brought back to Rome. Bread became very popular as an alternative to the ubiquitous grain porridge. The Romans imported Greek bakers for hundreds of years, as they were considered especially good at their trade.

Miller-baker guilds were established during Emperor Augustus. There were hundreds of bakeries in Rome that made bread for the citizens. This bread was given away for free to keep the population calm. The Roman emperors ensured their popularity by offering "bread and circuses".

In the ninth century there were bakers throughout Charlemagne's empire, and a couple of hundred years later they were found throughout Europe. The master baker's symbol was now the pretzel, and there was strict control to prevent the bakers from tampering with the weight of bread.

Night work has always been the norm. In France the bakers started early in the morning. They slept on bags of straw when they were not working. Food and lodging was provided by their masters. Working the dough was hard and the ovens were hot. In the mid-19th century the bakers in Central Europe went on strike demanding better working conditions and their own beds to sleep in.

Historically, bakers have been few in Sweden since most people lived in the countryside and made their own bread, but as the cities grew so did the number of bakeries with German and Danish bakers arriving to work in Sweden. People in the cities did not have access to large ovens to the same extent as they did in the countryside.

During the 16th century, there were so many bakeries in Stockholm that a bakers' guild was established to regulate the price of bread and set standards for the training of apprentices and masters. The first "pretzels" and sweet cream buns (*semlor*) were made in 1679. White "French" bread did not arrive until a hundred years later.

Modernizing the bakeries

Modernization of the bakeries started in the 19th century. Mechanical mixers took over the heavy work, and as industrialization picked up speed, competition increased and special steam-powered bakeries were built.

Most small bakeries closed down after the Second World War, but a few turned into large industries that were forced to produce vast amounts of bread at a low price. The old methods using starters, scalding and long proving times were no longer efficient.

The baking machines were slow, and more powerful mixers were introduced for smoother doughs and higher breads. At the same time, various additives wre used to speed up production. Germany and the Netherlands were at the forefront in this respect. These additives reduced proving times, but at the expense of flavour and texture.

The most common additives are mono- and diglycerides present in natural fat. Ascorbic acid aids the production of phosphates and strengthens the gluten. Ascorbic acid is present in all rising agents, and is added to flour to improve baking qualities. In other European countries a little or no ascorbic acid is added to the flour.

When I began my apprenticeship in the 1960s, patisseries were starting to make bread. I remember that we made fine farmers' loaves, wort loaves, wholemeal loaves and, of course, white "French" bread. In those days bakers had lower status than pastry-cooks, and most of the patisseries would not make bread. The industry was inundated with flour mixes, and the future lay with the semifinished products manufacturers. The result is obvious, there are very few bakeries and patisseries left.

Fresh high-quality bread

When I was a boy there was a patisserie in every neighbourhood, and fresh bread was always available. Today, many people rely on bake-offs from their local supermarket, which at least provides some of the joy of eating fresh bread.

On the Continent people often buy bread several times a day. This is why bakeries in France, where more bread is consumed than anywhere else in the world, make a batch of bread every hour. In Sweden, we have a wide range of different types, but most are wrapped in plastic and are spongy and sweet.

In France they use a form of natural sourdough starter, levain, combined with long proving times, with a better quality and taste as a result. If the baker displays a sign saying "Artisan boulanger" you can be certain that he knows what he is doing and that the bread is made in-house. *Travail pour levain* means that the baker uses traditional methods. You often also see the caption "pur beurre", which means that real butter is used.

At a praline-making course at the Richemont school in Luzern, I got to know a Frenchman who owned a bakery and patisserie in Paris, the Pâtisserie Glacerie Chocolaterie Dupont, and I went off to Paris to learn more about French baking culture. Once there, I encountered an old-fashioned and uncompromising dedication to making high-quality products daily.

In my view, the French are best in the world at making bread, when it comes to quality as well as upholding old traditions. I have myself contributed by writing a series of articles in the trade magazine Bread & Cakes in which I describe how you can use various recipes in the old, traditional way instead of relying on industrial short-cuts.

Bakers in Switzerland also make high-quality bread and cakes, and each kanton has its regional variation. When I was working in Switzerland, the bakeries and patisseries were always full of customers from as early as six in the morning. The offered breakfast with freshly made croissants as well as the typically Swiss *gipfeli* and *weggli*. Austrian, German and Danish bakeries have unfortunately become rather like the ones in Sweden, that is to say industrial enterprises using semifinished products and powdered sourdough. There are of course exceptions in both Germany and in Austria where you can find many artisan bakers. Patisserie Lenôtre is established throughout Germany, for

example. They make bread the old-fashioned way using natural soudough.

In Norway too, they are beginning to turn away from industrially made bread. The Åpent bakery in Oslo, Gott Bröd and many others have started up in several locations, making and selling sourdough bread, and in Copenhagen there are a couple of bakeries that use only levain.

Italian bakers make wonderful sweet bread with levain, for example panettone. The bread stays fresh much longer compared to bread made with yeast.

The salt-free bread that is served in many restaurants in Italy is mostly used for wiping up the sauce on your plate. There are many delicious Italian breads: *ciabatta*, *pilore* and round, fluffy sourdough breads. After I completed my training in Switzerland I asked the manager of the Coba Institute, Julius Perlia, if he could help me find an internship. As it turned out, he was able to help me, and I got a place at the famous Pasticceria Motta in Milan that specialized in *panettone*, a wonderfully light and fluffy bread. I also learned about various proving methods. In Italy they use an apple-based starter, just as I do in this book.

In the United States there is a large association of artisan bakers. Amy Scherber, who runs a number of bread shops in New York, worked for three months at three bakeries in Paris. Back in New York she opened a shop selling breads based on natural sourdough and levain. Through a glass pane you can watch the bakers at work. People throughout the United States have started to refuse to buy mass-produced bread, and quality bakers have opened all over the country. Most of these make bread with long proving times, between 16 and 18 hours in the fridge.

Good mealtime bread

I learned a lot during my first summer at Hotel Kramer in Malmö when I was fourteen years old. The restaurant was usually packed, and everything was made in the hotel kitchens. Apart from a restaurant kitchen and a cold buffet kitchen there were a bakery and a pastry kitchen that made all the breakfast rolls, bread, cakes and desserts. There was a special German oven in which you could bake directly on the hearth.

When I later started at the Savoy in Malmö, we bought most of our bread from various bakeries. We had breakfast rolls delivered in the morning, but made our own Danish pastries, croissants and bread rolls for lunch.
The main course did not include bread, and to the consternation of foreign guests, the staff would remove the bread basket as soon as the food arrived.

Nowadays, guests expect not only a delicious main course, but also high-quality bread, and wine that is served at the right temperature.

Bread has always been important feature of my guest appearances at restaurants, even though the main attraction is normally the dessert. I remember once at the Bomans restaurant in Trosa when the guests could smell freshly made bread all day in the dining room. Everyone loved it.

I will never forget when Magnus Johansson and I were travelling to Gothenburg to make sourdough bread with our old friends Håkan Thörnström of Thörnströms kök and Bengt Sjöström of Restaurang Linnéa. The sourdoughs were rising on the train and we had many good laughs, and in the end we had some wonderful bread.

One of the first Swedish chefs to realise the importance of serving good bread with food was the legendary Tore Wretman. In his book *Matminnen* (Memories of Food), he wrote that he had always thought that the quality and range of Swedish bread was rather boring compared to French baguettes and farmers' loaves. He also says that he remembers the bread rolls he bought at school – the crust was crisp and crackled, and the interior was so light and fluffy it was almost as if it was not there at all.

Nice *breakfast rolls* are made by making a loose basic dough containing 1,700 g white flour per litre milk, 60 g fresh yeast, 35 g salt and 25 g sugar. Leave the dough to prove for 60 minutes. Knock it back a couple of times. Roll out the dough and tear off roll-sized pieces. Place these with the cut side down, on a floured work surface. Cover with a tea-towel and leave until doubled in size. Turn them over with the floured side up and place them in the oven with a little steam. Bake until very crisp (for times and heat, see French bread, p. 63). Splash some water over the rolls as you take them out of the oven to create a nice, crackled surface.

Örjan Klein and Björn Halling are two colourful individuals who have produced a great bread recipe for Restaurangakademien (The Restaurant Academy).

Bread as it is made by the Restaurant Academy
This is a simple recipe for very good bread:
Take 1 l of water, 25 g fresh yeast and 1 kg white flour. Work the dough vigorously for approximately 15 minutes. Add 30 g sea salt and increase speed. Work the dough until it no longer sticks to the side of the bowl. Leave it to prove for 60 minutes. Use a little flour to gently turn out the dough on the baking tray without destroying the gas bubbles. Leave to rise for 60 minutes and bake until crisp on the outside (time and oven temperature as for Ciabatta, p. 171). This bread is tasty, light and fluffy.

There are many different bread types in Sweden, for example round rye cakes, hole cakes and loaves sweetened with syrup. Then there is crisp bread from Dalarna, soft and hard crisp bread from the north of Sweden and hearth bread, wheat cakes and fisherman's cakes from the west coast. Many of these are too sweet for my taste. The bread from the southern province of Skåne is often scalded and moist. Sweet and sour bread and dark rye bread are typical of this region.

As I wanted proof of competence, I naturally graduated as a master baker as well as a master pastry chef. There was no master baker working in Malmö twenty years ago, which meant that the bakers' association had to bring in one from Gothenburg and one from Värnamo. There was no problem when it came to the pastry chef examination, however, as the master pastry chefs Hans Eichmüller and Calle Widell both worked in Malmö.

Baking in a Stone Oven

It has again become popular to use stone ovens for baking bread, and bakers are beginning to appreciate the value of using traditional methods. At Olof Viktors bakery in south-east Skåne most breads take three days to make. The first day, various starter mixtures are set to rise overnight. On the second day, the dough is kneaded (see p. 33), after which it is left to prove in large plastic boxes with lids for one to three hours. After that the doughs are divided up and the loaves are shaped. Most loaves are put into floured proving baskets or on baking trays and are left to rise for approximately sixteen hours, until the following day. This slow process gives the bread a strong aroma as well as the right acidity and texture.

We stoke the oven with seventy-five kilos of firewood after lunch and it is hot enough to use during the night, when our bakers get to work. The temperature is nearly 300°, so

sometimes the first batch is destroyed. In order to prevent this happening, we cover the floor of the oven with tin plates. No steam needs to be added since the heat is naturally moist, which gives the bread its distinctive flavour.

At home you can emulate this process by buying a 2–3 cm thick stone slab that fits into the oven. Heat the stone well and put the bread straight on it or on a pre-heated baking tray, and the bread will instantly get a better height.

I usually spray water into the oven with a flower spray to add moisture, it softens the surface of the bread, which gets higher and more light and fluffy. When the loaves are ready I place them on a wire rack to cool and give them a quick spray of water to make the crust crack up. Traditionally, bakers would baste the bread as it came out of the oven with a brush dipped in water. To make them cool down more quickly, place them on a wire rack or in spacious baskets, as they do in France.

Ingredients

Bread is an important part of everyday life. It is a combination of the four elements: earth, fire, air and water. The seed is put into the earth, it grows and it germinates. The rain and the sun ripens the grain and you need fire to bake the bread – no fire, no bread. Being able to control the fire in a stone oven or to switch on an electric oven are essential preconditions for baking.

Bread-making originated in the Middle East and was probably developed from various types of porridge. Wheat and barley were cultivated in the Eufrates and Tigris valleys about 9,000 years ago. The first breads were made from barley, a gluten-free cereal grain. These were flat since gluten is necessary for the rising process.

Types of cereal grain
The grains from which we make our bread all belong to the grass family. The most commonly used grains in the Nordic countries are wheat, rye, barley and oats.

WHEAT (*Triticum*)
The wheat family includes twenty species. The cultivated species were derived from wild grasses. The cultural history of wheat is disputed and complex. The most common grain in ancient Egypt was emmer wheat (*Triticum dicoccum*),

which is still cultivated in, for example, Turkey. Another species is durum wheat (*Triticum durum*), which is very high in protein, Polish wheat (*Triticum polonicum*), spelt (*Triticum spelto*) and common wheat (*Triticum aestivum*).

Common wheat, or bread wheat, is now the dominant crop and the most important grain in the world. The wheat harvest follows the sun from the northern to the southern hemisphere. High-protein wheat, i.e. strong or hard wheat, is cultivated in Canada, the United States, Russia and Argentina.

The wheat kernel contains gluten. This is why this is the most suitable grain for baking. During kneading the proteins absorb water to produce a sticky and elastic dough. The gases created by the yeast are retained, which makes the dough rise.

In Sweden both autumn and spring wheat are cultivated. Spring wheat is classified as the better-quality crop since it normally contains a high level of protein.

Durum is a hard, yellow and glossy wheat, rich in protein (14%). Swedish durum is cultivated on the island of

Top, oats and rye; centre, barley and wheat; bottom, spelt (dinkel)

Ven, but most is imported. It is normally used for making pasta, but also some Italian breads. Durum wheat has excellent baking properties and can be bought either coarse ground or fine ground.

Spelt or dinkel is an ancient form of wheat. Dinkel flour is marketed in several grades (kernels, white, whole-grain, etc.). It has a strong flavour and makes very good bread. Dinkel can be found in health food shops. It is cultivated on the island of Gotland and a few other places in Sweden.

Kamut, now classified as Triticum polonicum, is an old-fashioned form of wheat that has gained in popularity in the UK and the United States. It has a strong, rustic flavour.

RYE (Secale cereale)

Rye is a relatively new grain, probably originating in the Middle East. The grains are greyish green and narrow. Rye is better suited to the cold than wheat and is an important crop in countries with cold climates. Rye is mostly used in rye bread and mixed grain bread, a combination of wheat and rye. The baking properties are not as good as for wheat, but it becomes easier to handle if you add sourdough. The pentosanes present in the flour swell, improving the baking properties.

BARLEY (Hordeum sativum)

Barley comes from north-east Africa. It is the most commonly cultivated grain in Sweden. A small amount is made into flour (used in flat breads from northern Sweden), but most of the harvest goes to breweries.

OATS (Avena sativa)

Oats is a cereal grain originally from south-eastern Europe and the Orient. It contains important minerals and vitamins, but lacks gluten. If you use oatmeal for baking, it should be scalded first.

MILLING

The production of flour is a complex process. During milling, the grain is broken down and the different components separated. Wholemeal flour is made from the whole grain, in other millings the outer husk and the germ – rich in protein, vitamins and fat – are removed. The remaining kernel is 85% of the grain, and this is where the starch is found. White flour is made from the endosperm. In Sweden we use mainly wheat, rye, oats, and barley.

Flour should be kept in a dark, cool and dry place. With long time storage, it loses moisture, fat and sometimes weight.

TYPES OF FLOUR

Below is a description of the most common flours suitable for baking:

- Use strong, that is to say protein-rich, unbleached flour for making white, fluffy, light bread; or, if you prefer, a protein-rich stoneground flour.
- Whole wheat flour is a flour from which only the husk and part of the germ have been removed. It is darker, contains more fibre and protein than regular wheat flour and has a more distinctive flavour.
- Most organic mills use no additives while the larger, more industrial mills add amylase (for improving baking properties in wheat), ascorbic acid, iron and vitamin B to their products.
- Plain white flour does not have the same baking properties as whole-meal flour. I normally use extra fine flour with a lower gluten content for cakes and pastry, biscuits, shortbread and sponge cakes.
- Professional bakers and chefs use extra strong wheat flour with 10, 11 and up to 13.5 per cent protein. These are most suitable for making bread. Sweet wheat doughs are normally made using flour with a 10 per cent protein content, but I prefer a stronger flour for this type of bread too.
- Extra coarse whole wheat flour is nice and rustic, with around 10% protein. It is a well-flavoured flour made from the whole grain. Bran, wheat germ and crushed wheat all improve the flavour and texture of wholemeal breads.
- Then there is rye flour, fine or coarse, with a protein content of around 8%. Crushed or chopped rye, etc. are suitable additions to whole-grain bread or can be used as topping. Rye flour has a strong flavour and aroma, as opposed to wheat, which is more neutral in taste.
- Various flour blends are available on the market, for example, Shipton Mill's 5-seed blend containing malted wheat flakes, barley flakes, sunflower seeds, millet and oats. Personally, I seldom use ready-made flour blends – I prefer to mix my own.
- There is a whole range of other types of flour that are used in baking but do not contain gluten. These are usually added to give thet bread a more interesting texture or flavour. Examples include white, blue and yellow cornmeal, polenta and semolina, chestnut flour, rice flour, artichoke flour, peameal, buckwheat, etc., the list goes on. Add them to the dough for a more interesting or different flavour and texture, or sprinkle on top of the bread for a more attractive look.

Flour contains starch in the form of tiny granules. These granules consist of a nucleus and an outer layer. The outer layer absorbs water causing the granules to swell. At 30°C, they burst and become sticky.

Baking liquids

Water is the most common baking liquid. You can also use wort, beer, puréed vegetables, milk, yoghurt, cottage cheese, buttermilk, etc. They all have their pros and cons, but what is important to know, is that because all these liquids are more viscuous, they require less flour than a dough made with water. See p. 27 for temperatures.

WATER

Apart from flour, water is the most important ingredient in bread. The water dissolves the gluten in the flour, which is necessary for making the starch in the gluten sticky. Tap water is normally clean and of a sufficiently high quality to use, but leave the tap running for a few minutes to avoid any contamination.

MILK, YOGHURT, COTTAGE CHEESE

Milk produces a softer, denser bread with small pores that browns quickly in the oven. You need to use less flour when baking with milk. Milk is used for making sweet wheat doughs, tea bread, sausage, hamburger and sandwich breads. I always use full-fat milk when I am baking. Sometimes I use yoghurt, since it improves baking properties resulting in a large, well-risen bread. Cottage cheese makes the bread nice and moist, and it stays fresh longer.

Salt, sugar, fat and flavourings

SALT

The purest salt is ordinary table salt with 99.99% sodium chloride (NaCl). This is also called rock salt, which is mined from vast underground salt deposits. Another major source of salt is the sea, where the salt is extracted through evaporation. Gourmet salt is seawater that has been boiled in huge vats until only the brittle salt crystals remain. I prefer sea salt and normally use 20 g of salt per kilo of flour.

Salt has many functions in a dough. It improves flavour, elasticity and moisture retention, and slows down the proving process. Salt added at the end of the kneading makes the dough more elastic and the interior and crust whiter. If you use too little salt, you get a looser dough that is less elastic, sticky and less able to trap the gases.

The bread gets flatter, paler and the flavour bland. If you use too much salt it loses its shape, becomes moist and rises more slowly. It also browns too quickly in the oven and the taste becomes too salty.

SUGAR

Caster sugar consists of fructose and glucose molecules that are water soluble. The yeast feeds off the glucose while the fructose stays in the dough, influencing the colour of the bread. A little sugar speeds up proving while a large amount slows it down. Sugar is used to sweeten bread doughs and for a browner crust. Demerara, muscovado and other cane sugar types all flavour the bread in different ways.

HONEY

Different kinds of honey also add flavour and improve rising properties. Honey can be used instead of malt when cooking at home.

SYRUP

Syrup contains 80% dry substance, the rest is water. Ten centilitres of syrup weighs 140 g. There are many types – white, golden, brown or malt syrup are all readily available in the shops. Many Swedish breads contain syrup, especially the moist, dark, sweet-tasting breads from the south of Sweden.

MALT

Malt is one of the most ancient baking agents made from malted grain. It adds flavour and can improve baking properties in "weaker" flours.

EGGS

One egg yolk weighs approximately 20 g, an egg white approx. 30 g, a whole egg about 50 g and an egg including its shell about 60 g. Make it a habit always to weigh the eggs as they are very different in size. The lecithin present in the egg yolk helps distribute the fat and makes the dough elastic and able to retain the gases. Fluffy doughnuts and "Karlsbad" doughs should be made with the yolk only. Danish pastries, croissant and brioche doughs contain whole eggs, which helps to distribute the fat. Breads made with eggs dry out more quickly, therefore they should always be eaten fresh.

BUTTER

Always add the butter at room temperature when making sweet wheat doughs. The solid fat binds more air in the dough, improving rising properties and the dough becomes more pliant and elastic. The air bubbles grow larger during rising and baking, and the bread's volume increases. Never use melted butter even though many cookery books advise it. Melted butter absorbs more flour than soft butter, resulting in a heavier bread. Add the butter, a little at a time, after a few minutes' kneading. This improves elasticity and volume. Butter gives a denser texture and a wonderful aroma. Never substitute butter with margarine – it neither sounds or tastes very nice!

OIL

Olive oil is added to add a Mediterranean flavour to bread. The oil makes the interior denser and more chewy. Liquid fat makes the bread more tender, but smaller in volume because it lacks fat crystals, which reduces gas retention.

HERBS, SPICES AND OTHER FLAVOURINGS

You can flavour bread with anything you like. Here is a selection of my favourites: dried fruit (e.g. apricots, apples, prunes), paprika, potato, rhubarb, glasswort, seaweed, algae, salami, ham, sausage, coriander, sunflower seeds, ginger, star anise, cardamom, saffron, aniseed, fennel seed, cinnamon, allspice, Seville orange peel, nutmeg, tonka beans, vanilla, lemon, orange, lime, chilli, caraway, sesame seeds, poppy seeds, dill, parsely, thyme, oregano, basil, rosemary, lovage, nettles, chives, spinach, tomato, sundried tomato, garlic, olives, walnuts, hazelnuts, pistachios, coconut, raisins, almonds, muscovado sugar, parmesan and mixed cheese, syrup, honey, oil (e.g. truffle oil), vegetables, fruit, mushrooms (fresh or dried), currants.

Rising agents

All risen doughs contain yeast. Proving is a complex yet simple phenomenon. After adding yeast, lots of gas bubbles form in the dough, which makes it increase in volume. There are two types of rising agent, natural and chemical. These must be explained separately since they have different properties.

It is interesting to learn that fermented bread was baked as early as 6,000 years ago, probably an invention made by the ancient Egyptians. No doubt, someone left a mixture of flour and water too long. Microscopic fungi were mixed into the dough which, to the delight of the baker, started to rise. Then, he probably mixed this with new flour and water, and the new dough became tasty, light and aromatic. For this invention he must be blessed for all eternity by the patron saint of bakers, Saint Honorius.

FRESH YEAST

Yeast fungi (*Saccharomyces cerevisiae*) are found everywhere in nature, and natural yeast consists of micro-organisms that themselves feed, reproduce and eliminate waste products.

These micro-organisms were not observed until 1680, under a microscope. Later, it was the breweries that delivered "brewer's yeast" to the bakeries. Louis Pasteur then developed the type of yeast that we use today. Commercial fresh yeast contains some 10 billion yeast cells per gramme. When the yeast is added, the dough starts to feed off the sugar, proteins and nitrogen-rich substances that are produced and develops carbon dioxide gas that makes it rise.

Yeast needs liquid food, e.g. water. It also needs to be activated by the addition of heat. The ideal temperature is 38°C. Temperatures below 20°C and above 40°C slows down the fermentation process, and at 45°C the yeast dies.

Yeast is a unicellular fungus that, with the right nutrition, reproduces via a bud that separates from the mother cell, forming a new, separate cell that in turn reproduces by the same process. The yeast cells require energy, which they get from sugar-digesting enzymes. This process is also dependent on oxygen, which is taken from the air. As the yeast metabolizes, carbon dioxide (which "lifts" the dough), water and heat are produced. The fungi reproduce during kneading (when oxygen is added).

The ideal dough temperature is 24–28°C. Many cookery books recommend that you heat the liquid to 37°C. This is true if you are kneading by hand. It takes between 20 and 30 minutes to work a dough until it becomes very elastic by hand, and it is hard to achieve the right friction with cold water or water at room temperature.

If you are using a kitchen assistant with dough hooks, friction increases the dough's temperature to 24–26°C during kneading. If you then heat the liquid, the temperature will get too high, the dough will rise too quickly and the flavour will suffer. Never allow the dough to get warmer than 28°C.

Always store fresh yeast in an air-tight container in the fridge.

DRY YEAST

Store dry yeast in a dry place. Dry yeast contains between 4% and 6% water. It is practical and easy to have at home, but I prefer fresh yeast since I find that the result is better. The baking liquid must be heated to 45–50°C to activate dry yeast.

CHEMICAL RISING AGENTS

Examples of chemical rising agents are baking powder, bicarbonate of soda, ammonium carbonate, potash and soda. Chemical rising agents react quickly in contact with water and produce carbon dioxide. They are suitable for some types of dough such as soda bread.

Natural yeast reproduces during the entire proving process and constantly increases in volume. Chemical rising agents are consumed rapidly after they come into contact with water. Adding too little yeast, not mixing the dough in the right way or not giving the yeast a chance to react the way it should are all factors that influence the end result. There is a distinction between bread and soft products made with biological yeast and sponge cakes, Swiss rolls, cake bases, meringues, etc. that are made with chemical rising agents, whereby air is added during whisking, introducing bubbles into the batter.

Chemical rising agents (baking powder, ammonium carbonate, bicarbonate of soda) are added to soft cakes made with a lot of fat to make them rise in the oven. Ordinary yeast does not work with large amounts of sugar and fat.

PROVING AND PROVING TIMES

After the dough has been kneaded and it is time to leave it to rise, you should not cover it with a tea-towel, as is usually recommended. As it allows the passage of air, the dough can easily dry out on the surface. Instead, leave it in a lidded plastic container that holds about 10 litres. Oil it lightly with a neutral food-grade oil, unless the recipe

Maria Olsson with a "mother", or "chef" starter for bread made with levain.

says otherwise. The oil prevents the dough from sticking to the container, improves rising and makes it easier to turn out.

It is in fact the amount of yeast and the proving time that determine the flavour and aroma in the finished bread. The shorter the rising time, the blander the flavour.

- A dough with 10–25 g yeast per litre of water needs to prove for approx. 3 hours to mature.
- A dough with 50–60 g of yeast per litre of water needs to prove for 60–90 minutes.
- A dough with 80–100 g yeast per litre of water needs to prove for 30–45 minutes.

Sourdough

The most ancient proving method uses wild yeast.

To put it simply, a sourdough is a mixture of flour and water that has been left so long that it starts to ferment; wild yeast is formed and starts to reproduce.

A sourdough is kept alive by the constant addition of new flour and water. It starts to form bacteria, lactic acid, lacto bacillae, acetic acid, aromatic substances and, in some processes, yeast. When a lactic acid bacterium is heterofermentative it means that it is able to produce both lactic and acetic acid. A homofermentative bacterium is only able to produce lactic acid.

Sourdoughs were originally only used as a rising agent. In Sweden, it is usually added for flavour and aroma. Commercial bakeries do not have the time to leave the dough to rise; instead they add commercial yeast in order to speed up the production of carbon dioxide and acid.

SOURDOUGH BREAD AND RYE ARE GOOD FOR YOU

Coarse bread made from sourdough and rye flour is a healthy alternative to white, fluffy bread, which has a negative effect on blood-sugar levels in the body. Sugar, or saccharose, is metabolized during fermentation, and the carbohydrates in sourdough and wholegrain bread are absorbed slowly into the blood stream. The acids that are formed during sourdough fermentation delay the breakdown and absorbtion of starch in the digestive system. In wholgrain bread, the starch is encapsulated, which prevents the enzymes from coming into contact with the starch. This slow process helps to stabilize blood sugar levels in the body, which is better for you health.

Wheat sourdough and rye sourdough

HOW TO GET STARTED

We are now going to make a sourdough. We begin by making two sourdoughs, one rye-based and one wheat-based, which I always do when I am making well-flavoured bread with lots of aroma. I have tried hundreds of different ways to make sourdough, and I have found that the following recipe works best for me.

Use untreated, unbleached rye or wheat flour depending on whether you want to make rye or wheat sourdough. The flour contains approximately 100 lactic acid bacteria per gram. Grated apple speeds up the fermentation process. Some use honey, grated raw potato, untreated grapes or raisins for a good quality sourdough that ferments rapidly.

This is my way of doing it:

DAY 1–3
200 g water (2 dl)
200 g rye or wheat flour
100 g grated apple

1. Mix water, 35ºC, with flour and grated apple in a stainless steel bowl. Pour into a 2 l glass jar with a lid.
2. Place the jar in a warm place, ideally 26–30ºC, for 3 days. If you have no such place at home, place the jar in an unheated oven. Speed up the process by stirring once a day.

DAY 4
Transfer this starter base to a large bowl. Add 200 g flour and 200 g (2 dl) water, 35ºC. Stir carefully with a ladle and leave for another 24 hours at the same temperature as before.

DAY 5
The sourdough is now ready to use. Store it in the fridge until needed.

Start by making both a wheat sourdough and a rye sourdough, and you will soon be able to make wonderful bread at home in your own kitchen or in a professional kitchen. Sourdough is not hard to make, it almost makes itself. Looking after a sourdough is almost like caring for a newborn baby!

When the sourdough is ready, the pH-value will be below 4, acid production will slow down and eventually cease altogether. The lactic acid bacteria live on, however, and will begin to reproduce if you add more flour and water.

Sourdough in reserve
Mix the sourdough with the same flour from which it was originally made until it is dry and crumbly. Turn out on a work surface and leave to dry for two days at room temperature. Store in jar in a dry place.

The next time you are baking with sourdough, take a small portion of the dry base and whisk in tepid water until you have a thick batter. Place the bowl in lukewarm water to start fermentation; it takes about 3–4 hours. Once it has started, add a bit more water and flour to activate. Cover with cling-film and leave to rise until the next day. The sourdough is now ready to use, and you can skip the second stage of preparation.

What are the advantages of baking with sourdough?
The bread becomes aromatic with a pleasant, dense texture and an elastic, moist interior. Sourdough bread is good for you, partly because it has a benefical effect on cholesterol levels. Tests have shown that diabetics can reduce their insulin levels by eating rye sourdough bread.

What goes on inside a sourdough?
In rye sourdoughs, the pentosanes present in the flour swell, which prevents the proteins from doing the same. The ability of the pentonsanes to bind water is important when you are making rye bread, since rye does not have the same ability to form gluten as wheat flour. A sourdough that has gone through all stages contains approximately one billion yeast cells per 100 g dough.

A loose dough that rises overnight in the fridge produces larger pores, like Italian and French breads. A stiffer dough results in a bread with finer pores like German bread. Swiss breads are somewhere in between.

Bread in Germany and Eastern Europe often has a tangier flavour than in the rest of Europe. The sourdough ferments at lower temperatures and is kept in the fridge, with the result that acetic acid bacteria take over, making the dough stiffer. French and Italian sourdoughs are milder, and sometimes the only way to deduce the presence of sourdough is the fine quality of the bread.

Baking with levain
RAISIN-BASED SOURDOUGH
Many bakers in France use raisins for starting a sourdough. The end result is the same whether you use raisins or apples to start fermentation. The raisin method is used for all breads made at the famous Lenôtre patisserie in Paris. In the United States, they often use untreated grapes or apricots for the starter.

DAY 1

1,000 g water (1 l)
500 g California raisins
250 g sugar
100 g set honey

1. Heat the water to 30–35°C. Measure the ingredients in a large glass jar with a lid. Mix the ingredients and shake the jar until the sugar has dissolved.
2. Place the jar in a warm place, approx. 26–30°C, to kick-start the fermentation, or place in the unheated oven, which works too, but it takes another day before fermentation starts. Leave for 4–6 days. Shake the jar once a day to speed up fermentation.
3. Fermentation is complete when the lid of the jar opens with a pop and the mixture smells of alcohol. Pour the raisins into a sieve and squeeze out the liquid with the side of a ladle. Store the liquid (the raisin yeast) in a jar in the fridge, where it will keep for several months.

AFTER 4–6 DAYS:

MAKING THE "MOTHER"
Take out:
125 g raisin yeast
175 g strong wheat flour, preferably stone ground

Mix raisin yeast and wheat flour and knead on low speed for 5 minutes. Place in a 2 l plastic container with a lid and leave to rise in a warm place or unheated oven for 4 hours. (If you do not want to make a mother using raisin yeast and wheat flour, you can instead use 200 g wheat sourdough, see above, and proceed in the same way).

MAKING THE "CHEF"
Return the dough to the bowl and add:
125 g water (1.25 dl)
175 g strong wheat flour, preferably stone ground

Knead for another 5 minutes and replace in the jar. Leave for 4 hours. You now have a "chef". The surface should be smooth and dry.

In Italy, where this technique is very common, they place the "chef" on a clean, floured towel and tuck under the edges like on a parcel (not too tight) and keep it in the fridge at a low temperature (2–4°C). The "Chef" develops much more slowly when wrapped in a towel than when kept in a jar. It keeps for approximately two weeks, depending on the temperature of the fridge.

BAKING WITH LEVAIN
In order to be able to use the dough as a starter, it needs to be activated by adding fresh water and flour. This natural sourdough, or levain, keeps for about a week in the fridge if it is stored in a plastic container. If you bake often, all you have to do is multiply the amounts and you will have levain at the ready for a whole week.

When you are making a bread that requires, for example, "400 g levain" you need to begin by doing the following the day before baking.

200 g "chef"
600 g water (6 dl)
1,080 g strong wheat flour, preferably stone ground, or 900 g fine rye flour if you prefer to make a rye levain

1. Cut off 200 g of the "chef" and place in a bowl together with water and flour. Knead for 5 minutes on low speed.

2. Place the dough in a plastic container with a lid that has been rubbed with a little neutral oil, see below. Leave to rise in a warm place or in the unheated oven, 5–6 hours, or until it has doubled in size.
3. The levain is now ready to use. Refrigerate leftover levain. Bread made using this method has a unique flavour and texture. It is well worth the trouble.

When using this book, you do not need to follow all the methods. Decide whether you want to use sourdough or raisin yeast, but do not use both at the same time.

It is most common not to mix commercial yeast and wild yeast. Dedicated sourdough bakers tend to use only wild yeast.

Levain

Poolish

Starters, Proving and Baking

Starters

The starter ensures a better aroma and texture, and the bread will rise better, resulting in a larger bread.

If you bake a lot you should always keep a starter in the fridge. It keeps for about a week wrapped in a tea-towel. Make a parcel to slow down sugar metabolism and avoid over-fermentation. In this book, most of the starters are made without salt to reduce rising times.

Doughs made with a starter are called indirect doughs.

WHITE STARTER
In France this type of starter is called *pâte à fermeté*:

The basic recipe is as follows: Make a very elastic dough with 500 g (5 dl) water, 750 g strong wheat flour and 5 g yeast. Add 20 g sea salt towards the end to control and slow down fermentation. Cover with cling-film and leave to rise for 6 hours (or at least 11 hours in the fridge). This method will ensure a wonderful aroma and better baking properties.

POOLISH
This method was invented by Polish bakers, hence the name. Journeymen bakers brought the custom to France where they started to bake baguettes with poolish in the 1920s.

This is a method that greatly improves the quality of your bread. Measure 500 g (5 dl) water, 500 g flour (any type) and approx. 5 g yeast or 50 g active sourdough in a bowl. Add water (35°C) and whisk until you have a batter, see picture below left. Cover with cling-film and leave to rise for 3–6 hours or overnight in the fridge. As you mix the batter with the other ingredients, the flour will have increased in volume, releasing a strong aroma. The bread is slightly tangy and light with a chewy, crisp crust.

STARTER 2
In some of the recipes (Wort Bread and Dark Rye Bread) I use a second starter to start the fermentation process. Wort and dark rye doughs are heavy and need the second starter for a moist, well-flavoured result.

SCALDING
Scalding is another type of starter that improves the quality of the bread.

Normally, the ingredients are 500 g (5 dl) water that have been brought to the boil and poured over various types of wholemeal flour, e.g. rye. The normal ratio is 250 g flour to 500 g (5 dl) water. Cover with cling-film and leave overnight. The temperature after mixing should be about 70°C.

This has the effect of allowing the dough to absorb more water, resulting in a moist and slightly sweet interior. This method is used for fine farmers' loaves, Laputa Bread, Sweet and Sour Bread and is typically used in breads from the southern province of Skåne.

LOW-TEMPERATURE SCALDING
Do not bring the water to the boil, but take it off the heat just before boiling point. This results in a bread with larger pores and great flavour. Cover with cling-film and leave overnight. The temperature of the mix should be around 50°C.

SOAKING
The soaking method is used for crushed wheat, rye and other crushed grains used for whole-grain bread. Soak the grain overnight in water no warmer than 50°C. If the temperature is higher, the starch will start to get sticky.

STARTER 3
This method is mostly used for Dark Rye Bread or bread with a very dense interior. Bring 500 g (5 dl) water to the boil and pour over 175 g rye flour. Cover in cling-film and leave overnight. The temperature of the mixture should be 85–90°C.

Kneading
MIXING WHEAT FLOUR DOUGHS
I have used an Electrolux kitchen assistant and a KitchenAid for kneading. Kneading by hand is fine, but it takes a long time to activate the gluten, and the quality and texture is not as good. A dough that has not been worked properly cannot produce enough fermentation gas.

Dissolve the yeast in the water. Pour the flour into to the bowl and add the starter if you are using it.

Mix on low speed to begin with, approx. 13 minutes, without salt. The water must have time to soak in, making the gliadin and glutenin swell to form gluten. Add salt and knead for another 7 minutes, i.e. a total of 20 minutes. Increase the speed during the last few minutes to stretch the gluten properly. For even better gluten formation, knead the dough for a few minutes before adding the fat.

Always add salt towards the end of kneading. The salt strengthens the gluten if added later in the process, resulting in a more pliant and elastic dough that is able to trap the gas. Always make an elasticity test (see p. 34) before finishing kneading.

MIXING RYE FLOUR DOUGHS
Knead slowly for about 15 minutes. Add salt after 5 minutes. The rye flour swells slowly and must have time to absorb the water. Rye has very different baking properties from wheat. It cannot form gluten and has a fairly high pentosane content. The pentosanes bind the water and swell in contact with sourdough. Therefore, I always use sourdough when I make rye bread.

When making dough with a mixture of rye and wheat, remember that the dough cannot be kneaded as intensely as a wheat dough since rye flour is weaker than wheat. If it starts to get glossy, it has been kneaded for too long. It can no longer trap the gases and begins to disintegrate.

Remember that all the flour should be at room temperature and added from the start, otherwise some of the flour will not be worked long enough, which impairs rising.

KNEADING
All the ingredients are mixed to form a dough and gluten is formed. During the kneading process, bubbles become trapped in the dough, ensuring a light and fluffy bread, and the gluten strings become stretched and elastic; but if you work the dough for too long, the gluten strings break and the dough collapses.

ELASTICITY TEST

It is important to check elasticity during kneading. Pick up a piece of dough and stretch it between your thumb and forefinger. The dough should form a thin, very elastic membrane. If fissures are easily formed you need to continue kneading, but if it breaks, you have worked it too long. It is difficult to determine when a rye dough is ready to use, since it feels sticky and stiff at the same time.

Elasticity test

ABOUT TEMPERATURES AND KNEADING

In many of the recipes an ideal dough temperature is provided. It is important that the baking liquid is at the right temperature.

- Always use cold tap water to slow down fermentation. When I make sweet wheat dough with milk, I take it straight from the fridge. The friction generated in the mixing or kneading process increases the temperature. Most wheat doughs should be kneaded for 20 minutes.
- Strong flour needs more vigorous kneading than weak flour in order to develop gluten.
- I normally work rye flour doughs for 15 minutes since they do not form gluten, but the temperature rises significantly anyway. It is always more difficult to determine when a rye dough is ready to use.
- The doughs usually reach a temperature of 24–26°C after kneading in an electric mixer. This is normally the ideal temperature, unless the recipe says otherwise.
- When you make fine baguettes, the dough must not get too warm and rise too quickly. Use very cold water and the dough will reach a temperature of 24°C, which is ideal.
- Always check the temperature of the dough!

CHECKING THE TEMPERATURE OF THE DOUGH

Do as professional bakers do and measure the temperature scientifically. It only takes a moment:

1. The recipe says 26°C. Multiply by two, which makes 52°C.
2. Measure the temperature of the flour. Deduct the flour temperature (20°C in this case) from the calculated temperature (52°C). 52 minus 20 is 32°C.
3. Add the bakery factor, 2°C for a cold bowl, i.e. 32 plus 2, which makes 34°C.
   For a dough with a temperature of 26°C, the water has to be 34°C.
   This is the full formula: (Desired dough temperature x 2) – flour temperature + bakery factor = water temperature.

I always use cold water when I bake without using a starter. If you want to calculate the temperature for an indirect dough, i.e. using a starter, you need to measure the temperature of the starter too in order to determine the water temperature.

First proving

Fold the dough like a cushion and place in a lightly oiled plastic container with a lid. While it is resting, the flour will swell, creating an elastic gluten network for stability. No proving means no elasticity, and the less yeast you use, the longer the proving time. Gluten is sensitive to acids

and may lose its elasticity if the dough is left too long. It will disintegrate and become unfit for baking. Low temperatures slow down acid formation, and the dough can be left to rise for much longer without turning sour.

It is therefore possible to leave the dough overnight and start shaping the breads first thing the morning. The gluten absorbs water during proving and acquires a dry surface, which is a sign that the dough is now mature and ready to use.

Rye doughs seldom need to prove for more than 60 minutes, or they start to collapse. When making a rye dough, you let the flavour and aroma develop in the starter, scalding or sourdough.

The dough needs to be left to rise for a minimum of 60 minutes and a maximum of 3 hours. If you need longer, it must be placed in the fridge or it will turn sour. During proving, acids are formed that react with the alcohol, which releases the aroma.

KNOCKING BACK THE DOUGH

This is normally only done with wheat doughs. Acetic acid is formed between 2°C and 25°C, which slows down the fermenting process. When you knock the air out of the dough, most of the acetic acid evaporates. Some remains together with the softer lactic acid to form aromatic substances. Place the dough on a work surface and use your hands to knock the air out of it. Fold the edges towards the centre to shape a cushion. Replace in the plastic container seam down, see picture 1–4 below. The traditional cushion shape makes the dough more pliable. The temperature ensures stability and provides the yeast cells with new nourishment.

The removal of carbon dioxide from the dough favours fermenting, the yeast propagates, the gas bubbles increase in number and the dough rises more quickly. By knocking back the bread you get a larger bread, which is easier to handle and which has a better and more elastic interior. Some doughs are knocked back twice, others three times. It makes loose doughs more stable.

SHAPING THE LOAF

Use kitchen scales when dividing the dough and make sure that all the individual loaves or rolls have the same weight. The pieces of dough are usually made into taut buns. The process is speeded up by using both hands.

Cover the dough with cling-film and leave to set for about 10 minutes. Shape a normal loaf by flattening the dough with your right hand and then folding it in three, see pictures 1–3 below. Seal the seam by knocking it down with your hand.

Round loaves are usually placed directly on the baking tray or on a floured tea-towel that is pulled up between the loaves to make them rise upwards rather than sideways, see picture on p. 36. You can also use proving baskets that have been dusted generously with flour. The baskets force the bread to rise upwards, which means that you can use rather loose doughs with large pores. Place the bread seam down in the basket if you want the bread to crack on top, or seam up, if you want a smooth surface.

1–4 Knocking back the dough

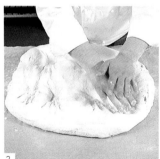

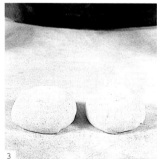

Making taut buns.

Bread rising on a floured tea-towel

If you prefer a bread with large holes inside, you need to be gentle with the dough and use the same technique as for baguettes: fold the dough gently in three, but do not squeeze the air out. Cover with a tea-towel and leave to set. Roll out the dough without applying pressure to avoid sqeezing out the air bubbles. When I make other types of bread I fold them carefully and place them in baskets seam down. This produces attractive loaves that crack in the oven.

It is not important to use both hands when shaping the buns, as the professionals do. The important thing is that you make them taut and even in size.

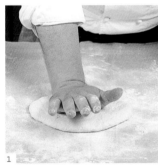

Shape the bread by flattening the dough and folding it in three. Knock the bread with your hand to seal the seam.

SECOND PROVING

In bakeries this is often done in a special room next to the bakery. The temperature in these rooms is normally 37°C and the humidity 70–80% to prevent the dough from drying out on the surface and to reduce rising times.

I only use this method for wheat doughs. These are rather heavy, but become light and fluffy if you let them rise properly. Brioche and "Karlsbad" dough, which are heavy, are well-suited to proving in an unheated oven.

Most breads need between 60 minutes and 3 hours for the second rising at room temperature. It all depends on the temperature of the room, and that is why I always state that the dough should double in size. At home you can leave it in an unheated oven and spray water over it with a flower spray to speed up fermentation and prevent it from drying out.

I nearly always leave the dough overnight in the fridge since the long rising time results in a wonderful aroma and texture. You can also leave the dough on a floured tea-towel and cover it with another towel (to prevent the surface from drying out). The traditional way, using a tea-towel, is ideal since it favours good volume and makes the bread rise slowly with a more attractive shape as a result. It is the same when you use proving baskets. Never increase the temperature during proving, it will produce an commercial-type loaf rather than an attractive, aromatic quality bread.

WHEN IS THE DOUGH READY TO BAKE?

This is something you get used to if you bake a lot. A bread that has risen for too long may collapse, lose its shape and form a hard, flat base. If it is left for too short a time, it tends to crack at the sides. Check that the bread is ready by prodding the dough to make sure it springs back.

Slash the bread with a special knife just before it goes in the oven. If you do it too early, the pattern will disappear. A sharp razor blade works fine too. The breads will open up in different ways depending on how you cut them. Cut deep, long slashes for baguettes to give them a characteristic look.

You slash the bread mainly for technical reasons, i.e. to distribute the tension throughout the gluten network so the bread can rise better in the oven. Some cuts are, however, purely decorative.

Baking

The purpose of this book is to show how you can make delicious bread at home using the same methods that we use at Olof Viktors at Glemminge. We make our bread in a wood-fired stone oven, just like the ancient Egyptians. We stoke it with 75 kg of wood every day. At home, you can emulate this method by purchasing a granite slab and rubbing it with plenty of food-grade oil to prevent the bread from sticking to the surface. Heat the stone to 250°C. If you cannot get hold of a stone slab you can use a heated baking tray instead.

After 5 minutes I lower the heat to 200° so that the crust does not get too brown. I quickly open the oven door after another 10 minutes to let in some dry air to ascertain a crisp crust. I usually repeat this a couple of times during the baking process since much of the flavour and aroma lies in the crust.

Place the risen bread directly on the hot stone or tray using a spatula. The professionals use a long baker's peel.

Spray water into the oven using a flower spray to emulate the moisture in a real stone oven.

For most of the recipes, I start off with a hot oven – 250°C. I preheat the stone or tray in the oven. After placing the bread in the oven I spray it with water to allow it to expand better and to soften up the surface. As the temperature rises, the gas bubbles increase, the pores get larger, the bread grows in height, and some of the gas evaporates into the oven.

Eventually the protein (albumin) in the gluten coagulates, and the bread forms a shell that gives off water to the starch cells. As the starch cells swell and become glutinous, the interior begins to set. To find out when the bread is ready, check the temperature. It should not be below 92–96°C for white and 96–98°C for heavier bread.

BAKING TIMES

I normally weigh the dough so I can calculate the time it needs in the oven.

- White loaf 400 g, approx 35–40 minutes.
- 500 g bread, approx. 45–55 minutes.
- 750 g bread, approx. 55–60 minutes.
- 1,000 g bread, approx. 75 minutes for a good crust.
- Baguettes need less time in the oven than a large bread, approx. 25–30 minutes.
- Danish pastries and croissants, approx. 15–16 minutes.
- Rolls, between 12 and 20 minutes, depending on type.
- The temperature should always be taken on breads made in tins.
- Flat breads should always be baked at a constantly high temperature or they will dry out.

I place most breads straight on a wire rack after removing them from the oven. I spray them with water for a crackled surface, which I find important in white breads.

CHECK THAT THE BREAD IS READY
Follow my time recommendations for crusty bread and use a thermometer if you are uncertain, especially for wholegrain bread.

Some people turn the bread over and knock it to check that it sounds hollow, but this is not a reliable test. The bread may be ready at the centre, but it may not yet have developed a full-flavoured crust.

Brushing and glazing
POTATO FLOUR GLAZING
Brush on hot bread to make it glossy.

Mix 10 g potato flour and 50 g water. Boil 200 g water, whisk in the flour mixture and bring to the boil.

I use this for Scalded Bread from Skåne and Swiss Weggli. It is also suitable for Sweet Loaf and Wort Bread.

EGG GLAZING
Whisk up egg and a little salt.

Always glaze sweet wheat dough, "Karlsbad" dough, Danish Pastries, croissants and brioches with egg once before proving and again before baking.

WATER
Brush with water to make grains and seeds stick to the dough, for instance poppy seeds on French rolls. You can also use milk, but then the bread will get browner.

BUTTER
Brush with butter after baking to enhance the flavour. Custard buns should be brushed with butter to make the sugar stick on top.

Storing the bread
I always store fresh bread wrapped in a towel at room temperature. It gives the crust a chance to breathe and the bread tastes good the day after too. White bread ages quickly.

Heavier scalded breads or those made with starters keep for up to a week without deteriorating.

Freezing and defrosting
Freeze the bread in plastic bags as soon as they have cooled down and defrost in the bag. Soft bread and bread with a crisp crust will be as good as fresh if you place them in the oven at 100°C for approx. 5 minutes for rolls and 8–10 minutes for loaves. Make sure that they are warm before taking them out of the oven. If you want a crisper crust, remove the plastic bag before defrosting.

Useful to know
- The amount of water used per kilo of flour is 600–650 g. In Sweden, we normally base our recipes on 1 l of water. In other countries they are often based on 1 kg of flour.
- French, Swiss and Italian doughs have a looser texture, which make them lighter and fluffier.
- Old flour desiccates and therefore absorbs more water, so always keep fresh flour at home. Add more water if the dough feels dry. Different mills make different quality flour. Look for your favourite brand.

"When using this book, you do not need to follow all the methods. Decide whether you want to use sourdough or raisin yeast, but do not use both at the same time."

WHITE BREAD

Three-strand plait

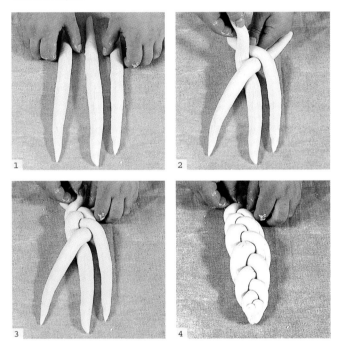

Four-strand plait

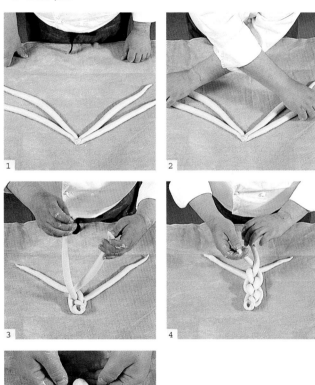

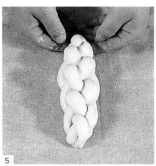

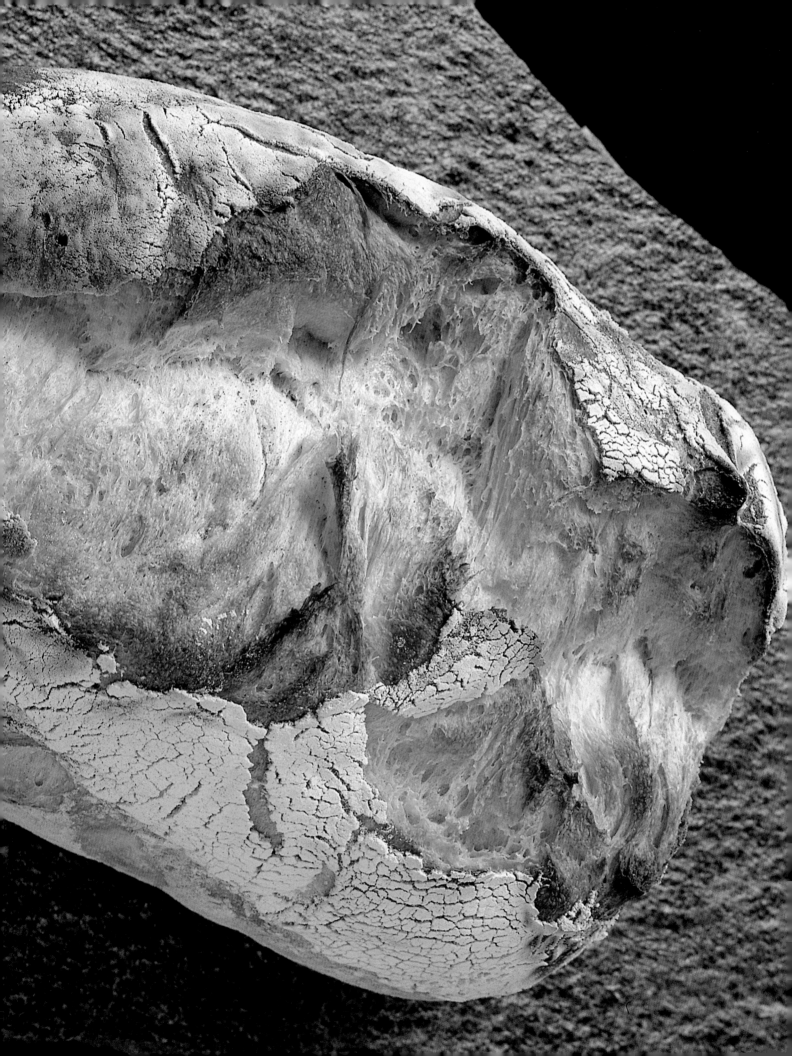

Plain White Bread from Olof Viktors

For this white, light and slightly tangy bread, which goes well with all kinds of food, you need to make a loose dough from strong flour. A great variation on this bread can be made with rye sourdough.

4 loaves
Ideal dough temperature 24°C

DAY 1

STARTER	KNEADING
2 g fresh yeast	15 g yeast
150 g water (1.5 dl)	500 g water (5 dl)
200 g strong wheat flour	1,000 g strong wheat flour
	350 g wheat sourdough
2 g salt	20 g sea salt

DAY 1
STARTER
1. Dissolve the yeast in the water, measure the flour into a bowl. Pour over the yeast mixture and knead the dough on low speed for 10 minutes.
2. Add the salt, increase the speed and work the dough for another 5 minutes.
3. Place in an oiled plastic container, leave in the fridge for 24 hours/min. 3 hours at room temperature.

DAY 1 OR 2
KNEADING
1. Dissolve the yeast in the water and pour over the wheat flour, sourdough and starter. Work for 13 minutes. Add the salt, increase the speed and knead for another 7 minutes until you have an elastic dough. Test for elasticity.
2. Place the dough in a lightly oiled lidded plastic container and leave for 60–90 minutes.
3. Sprinkle a thick layer of wheat flour on a baking tray. Quarter the dough without squeezing.
4. Gently fold into loaves. Place seam down on the tray.
5. Put in the fridge overnight, ideally 14–16 hours.
6. Preheat the oven with the stone or tray to 250°C.
7. Put two of the loaves in the oven and spray them with water.
8. Lower the temperature to 200°C after 5 minutes. After another 10 minutes open the oven door to let in some air. Repeat this procedure twice during baking for a crisper crust.
9. Bake for a total of 50 minutes. Take out the loaves and place them on a wire rack. Bake the other two.
10. Spray with water for a nice, crackled surface.

Suitable for freezing in plastic bags.

Italian Bread

This light, fluffy bread with a crisp crust goes well with all types of food. The dough gets extremely elastic due to the lecithin in the eggs, the gluten and the olive oil, which acts as a lubricant together with the gluten.

2 loaves
Ideal dough temperature 24°C.

POOLISH	KNEADING
5 g yeast	15 g yeast
500 g water, 20°C (5 dl)	25 g olive oil (0.25 dl)
150 g durum wheat	50 g egg (approx. 1 egg)
350 g strong wheat flour, preferably stone ground.	400 g strong wheat flour, preferably stone ground
	20 g sea salt

POOLISH
If you prefer to prepare the dough the day before you should leave the polish in the fridge overnight. If you would rather make it the same day, let it rest at room temperature for 3 hours.

1. Dissolve the yeast in the water. Add flour and beat into a thick batter. Cover with cling film.

KNEADING
2. Pour the poolish into a bowl, dissolve the yeast in the poolish using a whisk. Add the other ingredients except salt. Knead on low speed for 13 minutes until the dough is elastic. Add salt, increase the speed slightly and knead for another 7 minutes. Do not forget the gluten test by pulling the dough until a thin film forms. If necessary, continue until ready.
3. Place the dough in a lightly oiled lidded plastic container, leave it for 1 hour. Knock back the dough after half the time.

4. Place the dough on a lightly floured work surface and divide it into two equal parts.
5. Make two equally-sized balls and leave for 10 minutes.
6. Using durum flour, roll out the breads until they are the size of a dinner plate and fold over twice to shape a triangle. Sprinkle generously with durum flour. Apply pressure across the middle with a rolling pin.
7. Rise on a baking cloth dusted with flour until doubled in size, approx. 60–90 minutes.

8. Place the stone or tray in the oven and preheat to 250°C.
9. Slash the loaves as in the picture on p. 47.
10. Put the loaves in the oven using a spatula and spray with plenty of water.
11. Lower the temperature to 200°C after 5 minutes. After another 10 minutes open the oven door to let in some air. Repeat twice during baking.
12. Bake for a total of 60 minutes.
13. Take out the bread and cool on a wire rack. Spray them with water for a nice crackled crust.

This wonderful bread is suitable for freezing.

Tip
Making the poolish the day before saves time on the day of baking.

Italian Bread, various shapes, see p. 43.

French Baguettes with Poolish

This French national symbol has been made since 1920.

Using poolish (see p. 32) gives the bread a fluffy centre, a mild aroma and a crunchy crust. It is the formation of gliadin and glutenin in the poolish that gives the baguette its light and fluffy centre. Poolish originated in Poland in about 1840. Later, the method was introduced in Paris by Austrian itinerant apprentices, but it was not until 1920 that it was started to be used for making baguettes. This method gives the baguette its characteristic large holes.

4-5 baguettes
Ideal dough temperature 24°C.

POOLISH	KNEADING
5 g yeast	6 g yeast
300 g water, 20°C (3dl)	300 g water, 20°C (3dl)
300 g strong wheat flour, preferably stone ground	700 g strong wheat flour, preferably stone ground
	16 g sea salt

POOLISH
Mix the yeast and water in a 2 l bowl, add wheat flour and continue until smooth. Cover with cling-film and leave to rise for at least 4 hours at room temperature or overnight in the fridge. The poolish is ready when a cavity has formed in the middle.

KNEADING
1. Dissolve the yeast in the water, add poolish and wheat flour and knead the dough for 13 minutes on low speed. Add the salt, increase the speed and knead for another 7 minutes or until very elastic.
2. Place the dough in a lightly oiled lidded plastic container and leave for 90 minutes.
3. Cut off 350 g pieces. Fold the dough twice as in the picture on p. 192. Cover with a tea-towel and leave for 15 minutes.
4. Make thin baguettes by rolling the dough from the middle. Place seam up on a cloth sprinkled with flour and pull up folds between the baguettes to make them rise upwards. Leave to rise for 75 min. at room temperature or until doubled in size.
5. Preheat the oven to 240°C.
6. Turn the baguettes, one at a time onto a piece of wood or a ruler that is longer and wider than the baguette. Slash with a knife and place on the stone or tray. Bake in two batches.
7. Spray plenty of water into the oven.

8. Lower the temperature to 200°C after 5 minutes. After another 10 minutes open the oven door to let in some air. Repeat twice during baking.
9. Bake for a total of 30 minutes.
10. Take out the baguettes and place them on a wire rack. Spray them with water for a crackled crust.
11. Leave to cool and eat fresh.

NOTE. *The dough can also be left to rise in the fridge overnight.*

If you freeze the bread, remove the plastic bag and heat in a 100°C oven and it will be as good as fresh.

Pains régionaux

This French white bread can be made with the same dough and procedure as French Baguettes with Poolish, see p. 47, or White Bread with Levain, see p. 67.

Tricondo

Envelope

Comb

Round Flat Bread

Pistolet

Italian Bread

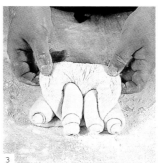

Le bâtard auvergnat

Shape a long loaf from 500 g of dough. Roll out a thin circle of dough and fold it over half way across the bread. See below.

L'auvergnat

Shape a round bread from 500 g of dough, roll out a thin circle from half the bun and fold it across.

Variation of Le bâtard auvergnat and L'auvergnat

Press the rolling pin across the middle of the dough, see pictures 1 and 2 below.

1

2

Variation with a "cap"

La tabatière

The same as above, but the top is slashed with a knife.

Pain Marguerithe

Several rolls are placed next to each other in the shape of a flower and sprinkled with flour, right.

Le bâtard

Short loaves slashed across the top.

Prepare and bake as French Baguettes with Poolish (p. 47) or White Bread with Levain (p. 67).
In France they leave the dough to rise at 14°C for 18 hours. You can also leave it in the fridge until the next day and then complete the rising at room temperature. This will result in very large holes inside.

NOTE. *If you want to make the bread the same day, rising takes approx. 75 minutes, but the holes get bigger if you let it rise overnight in the fridge.*

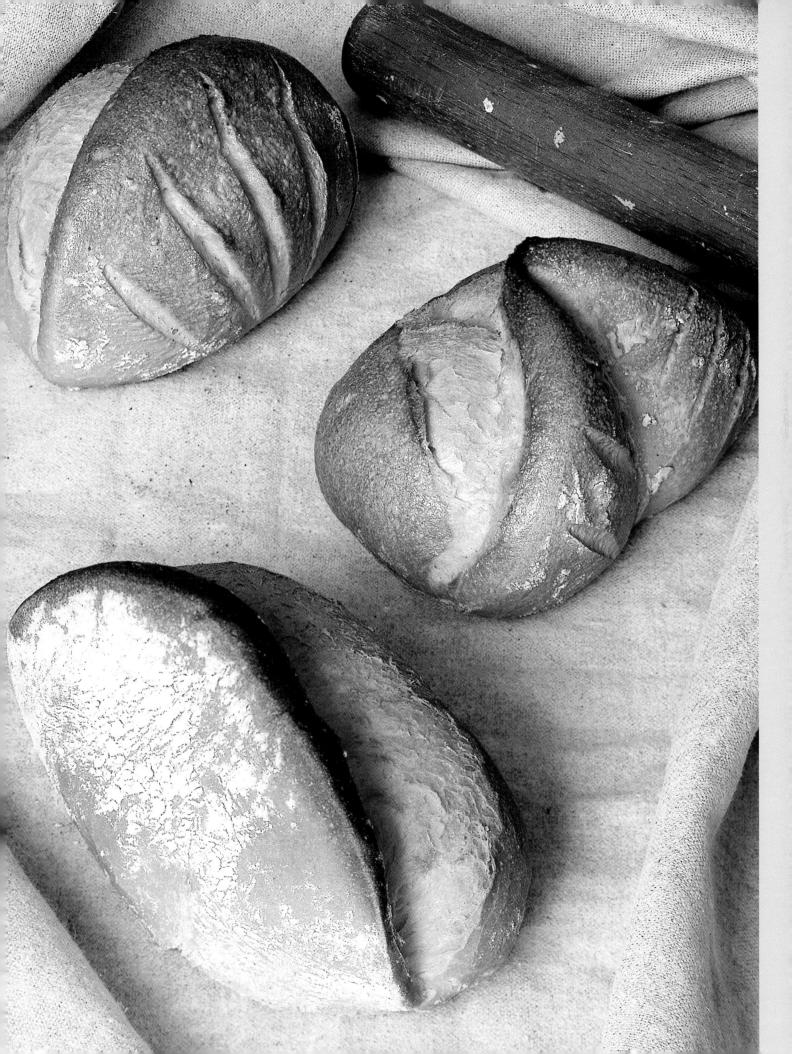

Garlic Baguettes

These garlic baguettes are delicious.

1 batch French Baguettes with Poolish dough (p. 47).

250 g butter	50 g parsley, chopped
30 g crushed garlic	salt and freshly ground
10 g lemon juice (2 tsp)	white pepper

Mix butter, garlic, lemon juice and parsley. Whisk until smooth, add salt and pepper to taste. Put the mixture in a tulle piping bag with a no. 14 nozzle. Squeeze out five lines the same length as the baguettes on a sheet of baking paper and leave to set in a cool place.

1. Divide the dough into five pieces and fold each in three. Cover and leave for 15 minutes.
2. Make rolls the same length as a baking tray. Place the butter mixture on top and roll into the dough.
3. Place seam down on a cloth sprinkled with flour. Leave to rise like a regular baguette.
4. Bake as regular baguette.

Wiener Kaisersemmeln

These work-intensive rolls with their gorgeous texture are served at the very best restaurants on the Continent. They were made in celebration of one of the Austrian emperors. At trade fairs, bakers often compete to see who is the quickest to fold them. The rolls get their distinctive texture partly through the folding, partly from the inclusion of milk.

Approx 25 rolls
Ideal dough temperature 26°

STARTER	KNEADING
15 g yeast	250 g full-fat milk (2.5 dl)
250 g full-fat milk (2.5 dl)	600 g strong wheat flour,
10 g set honey	preferably stone ground
250 g strong wheat flour,	10 g butter
preferably stone ground	18 g sea salt

STARTER

Dissolve the yeast in the milk, add honey and wheat flour. Knead on low speed for 10 minutes. Place the dough in a lightly oiled lidded plastic container and leave to rise for 90 minutes at room temperature. It is rather loose, and therefore it will rise quite high.

KNEADING

1. Weigh the milk, wheat flour and starter in the bowl. Knead for 3 minutes on low speed. Add butter and knead for another 10 minutes on the lowest setting. Add salt and knead for 7 minutes until the dough is very elastic. Test for elasticity.
2. Place the dough in a lightly oiled lidded plastic container and leave for 90 minutes. Knock back after half the time.
3. Place the dough on a lightly floured work surface and divide it into two. Roll and cut off 60 g pieces, use scales to get the exact weight.
4. Make rolls, cover and leave for 5 minutes.
5. Flatten the buns with your hand 2–3 times.
6. Use your right hand to fold the pieces towards the centre, repeat 5 times, finish by pressing a finger into the centre. See below.
7. Place the rolls folded side down on a cloth sprinkled

with flour, cover and leave to rise until doubled in size, approx. 45 minutes.
8. Preheat the oven to 250°C with the stone or tray.
9. Turn the rolls floury side up and place them in the oven. Spray water into the oven with a flower spray.
10. Lower the temperature to 200°C after 5 minutes. After another 10 minutes, open the oven door to let in some air. Repeat twice during baking for a crisper crust.
11. Bake for 18–20 minutes until golden brown.
12. Take out the bread and cool on a wire rack. Spray with water for a crackled surface.

German Brötchen

Use the same dough as for Kaisersemmeln (p. 52). I make rolls and use a rolling pin to press down the centre after they have risen for 15 minutes. Bake as for Kaisersemmeln.

I have made a quicker variation of this, where I fold the dough in three sections and leave to rise upside down, just like for Kaisersemmeln.

Can be frozen in plastic bags. Defrost in the oven and they will be as good as fresh.

Toasting Bread

These loaves are excellent for toasting or making sandwiches, and are very useful to keep in the freezer. I make oblong rolls and place them next to each other in order to break the gluten strings. The result is a softer interior than if you just place them whole in the tins. The same result can be achieved by making a plaited loaf.

4 loaves
Ideal dough temperature 24ºC.
4 2-litre loaf tins.

1,200 g strong wheat flour
30 g honey
60 g egg yolk (3 eggs)
50 g yeast
600 g full-fat milk (6 dl)
100 g butter
24 g sea salt

25 g butter for the tins
1 egg and a little salt for glazing

1. Weigh the flour in the mixing bowl together with honey and egg yolk. Dissolve the yeast in the milk and pour it over the flour mixture.
2. Knead the dough on the lowest speed for 5 minutes. Add the soft butter a little at a time. Keep kneading for 10 minutes. Add the salt and knead the dough until very elastic. Grease four loaf tins with butter.
3. Place the dough on a lightly floured work surface, divide into 20 pieces and make sausage shapes. Place these in four 2-litre loaf tins.
4. Place in an unheated oven and leave to rise until doubled in size, approx. 60 minutes. Spray a little water over them a few times to keep the dough moist so it can rise without cracking. Remove from the oven.
5. Preheat the oven to 230ºC and glaze the bread with the egg. Bake for approx. 35 minutes, lowering the temperature to 190ºC after 5 minutes.
6. Take out the tins and remove the loaves immediately. Return to the tray and bake for another 5 minutes to get a nice crust all round. Leave to cool on a rack.

Suitable for freezing.

Tip
This bread can be use for making sandwich layer cake. It is also suitable for hamburger and hot dog bread as the texture is very soft.

Toasting Bread (p. 53), Wiener Kaisersemmeln (p. 52) and German Brötchen (p. 53).

Weggli

This delicious Swiss bread is excellent for breakfast eaten with strawberry jam and accompanied by a café crème. (See picture on p. 56)

Approx. 25 rolls
Ideal dough temperature 27°C.

25 g yeast	1 egg and a pinch of salt
500 g full-fat milk (5 dl)	for glazing
10 g set honey	
900 g strong wheat flour, preferably stone ground	
100 g salted butter	
20 g sea salt	

STARTER
Dissolve the yeast in the milk, add honey and whisk in half of the flour to make a smooth batter. Cover with cling-film and leave to rise for 30 minutes.

KNEADING
1. Weigh the other ingredients and place in the mixing bowl, then add the starter.
2. Knead the dough for approx. 15 minutes on the lowest speed and test for elasticity. Increase speed and knead for another 3 minutes.
3. Place the dough in a lightly oiled lidded plastic container, leave for 60 minutes. Knock back after 30 minutes and repeat once.
4. Put the dough on a lightly floured work surface and divide into two. Roll out and cut off 50 g pieces.
5. Make perfectly round rolls.
6. Place the rolls on a cloth sprinkled with flour, pull up the cloth between the rows and leave to rise for 30 minutes. Take two rolls at a time and make a depression in the middle using a rolling pin. Roll a little at the centre of the rolls. The dough in the middle must not be broken, but should be wafer thin. Leave to rise for another 30 minutes.
7. Preheat the oven with the stone or tray to 230°C.
8. Place the rolls in the oven and spray them with water.
9. Bake for 12 minutes until golden brown.
10. Take out the rolls and glaze according to the recipe on p. 38. Leave to cool.

Tip
This dough is suitable for sandwiches and layered sandwich cake. For a coarser bread exchange 250 g of the wheat flour for wholemeal wheat or coarse rye flour. Also excellent for making spongy hot dog or hamburger bread. For hamburger breads: roll out 80 g pieces, make baps, brush with egg and dip in sesame seeds. Leave to rise and bake until golden brown.

Italian Cornetti

This is a wonderful Italian breakfast bread with a thick crust. When I studied at the Coba Institue in Basel I always used to buy it from the Conditorei-Bäckeri Bachman by the railway station.

Ideal dough temperature 24°C.

POOLISH	KNEADING
5 g yeast	10 g yeast
250 g water (2.5 dl)	250 g water (2.5 dl)
250 g strong wheat flour, preferably stone ground	850 g strong wheat flour, preferably stone ground
	10 g set honey
	50 g olive oil (0.5 dl)
	20 g sea salt

DAY 1
POOLISH
Dissolve the yeast in the water with a whisk and beat in the flour to make a thick batter. Cover with cling-film and leave for 24 hours at room temperature. This is important, as it will produces the typical tangy flavour.

DAY 2
KNEADING
1. Dissolve the yeast in the water. Add wheat flour, poolish and honey. Knead the dough for 3 minutes on the lowest speed. Add the oil and knead for another 10 minutes. Add the salt and knead for 7 minutes. Test for elasticity and increase the speed. Knead until very elastic.
2. Place the dough in a lightly oiled lidded plastic container and leave for 30 minutes.
3. Place the dough on a floured work surface and roll out long strands.

Top right, Tea Cakes (p. 199); centre, Zopf (p. 65); left, Sandwich Bread; bottom and right, Weggli (p. 55).

Cornetti

Make 40 g rolls and cover with a tea-towel. Leave for 15 minutes. Dust with flour and roll out into oblong shapes, about 1 mm thick, slightly thicker in the middle and thinner towards the ends. Roll into tight crescent shapes. Place one on a floured towel and press the other on top, pointing up. Leave to rise without cover for approx. 45 minutes. Proceed from point 4 below.

Mailänder

Make 80 g rolls and cover with a tea-towel. Leave for 15 minutes. Roll out in the shape of a long coil, approx. 1 mm thick and shape a tight crescent. Leave to rise as above and cut a deep slash through the centre just before baking. Proceed from point 4 below.

La main de Nice

1. Take 500 g pieces of dough that have been allowed to rest for 15 minutes covered by a tea-towel and shape into balls.
2. Roll out into long, flat strips, approx. 1.5 mm thick. Roll from both ends as for making croissants, press a rolling pin across the middle. Fold over and turn over (see p. 50).
3. Place the bread on a floured tea-towel and leave to rise until doubledd in size, approx. 45 minutes.

BAKING
4. Preheat the oven with the stone or tray to 250ºC.
5. Place the bread in the oven and spray plenty of water over them.
6. Lower the temperature to 200ºC after 5 minutes. After another 10 minutes, open the oven door to let in some air. Repeat twice during baking for a crisper crust.
7. Bake the Cornetti for approx. 18 minutes until golden brown. Start with the same temperature for all types of bread, but bake the La main de Nice for 35 minutes and the Mailänder for 45 minutes.
8. Take out the bread and place on a wire rack. Spray with water for an attractively cracked crust.

Slash the top with a sharp knife.

Sandwich Bread

Wittamer in Brussels make wonderful sandwich breads (opposite). Stefan Johnson Petersen, head of the bakery at the NK department store in Stockholm, finished off his training at this respected patisserie.

Approx. 35 rolls
Ideal dough temperature 26ºC.

40 g yeast	120 g sea salt
500 g full-fat milk (5 dl)	
1,000 g strong wheat flour, preferably stone ground	1 egg and a pinch of salt for glazing.
180 g butter	
50 g sugar	

1. Dissolve the yeast in the milk. Weigh the other ingredients and pour over the yeast mixture.
2. Knead the dough on low spead for 15 minutes. Test for elasticity, making sure that the dough is ready and very elastic.
3. Place in a lightly oiled lidded plastic container and leave for 45 min. Knock back after 20 min.
4. Turn out the dough on a floured work surface and divide into two. Roll out two coils using a little flour. Cut off 60 g pieces, make oblong rolls and put these on a baking sheet on a tray, approx. 12 to each tray. Whisk the egg and salt and glaze the rolls. Leave to rise for approx. 45 minutes. Glaze them carefully one more time.
5. Preheat the oven to 230ºC,
6. Bake for 12 minutes until golden brown.
7. Take out the tray and leave the bread to cool on a wire rack.

Tip
Lemon flavoured sandwich bread
Replace 50 g of the milk with fresh lemon juice and the finely grated peel of two washed lemons. Glaze with egg and dip in durum flour before rising and baking. Excellent with shellfish spreads.

Chocolate flavoured sandwich bread
Add 200 g roughly chopped dark chocolate, for example Valrhona Grand Cru Guanaja 70.5%, and 15 g finely chopped fresh peppermint leaves. Bake as plain sandwich bread. This is a children's favourite.

Crostini di formaggio

This Italian bread with a crisp, cheesy crust is great with food (see opposite page).

4 loaves

Dough as Cornetti, Italian bread, p. 55.

50 g smoked Italian salami, chopped
15 g chopped fresh basil

50 g + 100 g freshly grated parmesan cheese

1. Use the same dough as for Cornetti. Towards the end of the kneading add salami, basil and 50 g grated parmesan.
2. Divide the dough into four pieces, make four balls of dough and cover with a tea-towel. Leave for 10 minutes. Roll out into a long strip, approx. 2 mm thick, and shape a tight, short crescent, thicker in the middle and slightly pointed at the ends.
3. Leave to rise on a floured tea-towel. Pull up the cloth between the loaves, sprinkle with durum flour and cover. Leave to rise for 75 min.
4. Preheat the oven with the stone or tray to 250°C.
5. Slash the loaves across the top and sprinkle with 100 g parmesan.
6. Place two of the loaves in the oven and spray with plenty of water and put the remaining two in the fridge to prevent them from rising too much.
7. Lower the temperature to 200°C after 5 minutes. After another 10 minutes, open the oven door to let in some air. Repeat twice during baking.
8. Bake for a total of 40 minutes.
9. Put the loaves on a wire rack and spray with water for a crackled crust.

This bread goes very well with a Salade Niçoise on a warm summer day, but is not suitable for freezing.

Bunches of Grapes

This Italian specialty is sometimes made with a special truffle flour that is available in Italy. You use it to sprinkle over the bread instead of wheat flour. Ask for truffle flour the next time you are in Italy (opposite).

Add 10 g of truffle oil to a Cornetti dough (see p. 55), cut off 100 g pieces and roll these into balls. Place the loaves on a tray, not too close, as on the picture of the finished loaves.

Roll out a piece of dough, cut out leaves and place these over the top. Make a stalk and attach. Dust with wheat flour and rise uncovered for approx. 90 minutes until doubled in size. Bake as for La main de Nice, p. 57. Do not spray with water afterwards, it will destroy the crust.

Top, Bunches of Grapes; bottom, Crostini di formaggio.

French Rolls

Freshly made, flaky French rolls are a nice start to the day. Flaky rolls are readily available in our neighbouring country, Denmark. Unfortunately, the Swedish variety is usually chewy since we do not bake them long enough. Unless the table is covered in flaky crumbs after eating, they have not been made properly.

The "Danish" ingredient here is the egg yolk, which we do not normally use in Sweden for this kind of bread.

Ideal dough temperature 24–26°C
25 rolls or 4 loaves or 3 plaited loaves.

DANISH FRENCH BREAD DOUGH

30 g yeast	10 g honey
500 g water (5 dl)	25 g butter
950 g strong wheat flour, preferably stone ground	20 g salt
20 g egg yolk (1 egg)	

1. Dissolve the yeast in the water. Weigh flour, egg yolk, honey and butter in a bowl and add the water.
2. Knead the dough for 10 minutes on the lowest speed. Add the salt and increase the speed. Knead until very elastic for another 10 minutes.
3. Test for elasticity.
4. Place the dough in a lightly oiled lidded plastic container and leave for 60 minutes. Knock back the dough after 30 minutes.

For an even better result, make the starter the day before and leave to rise in the fridge for 24 hours.

STARTER

200 g water (2 dl)	360 g wheat flour
12 g yeast	8 g salt

Add the starter to the above dough (at stage 1) and the bread will become lighter and fluffier. Test both techniques and see if you notice the difference.

For a bread that tastes like Hungarian or Jugoslavian bread, omit the honey, egg yolk and butter, and reduce the amount of flour by 100 g. Also add the starter at the kneading stage.

Rolls

Roll out the dough using a little wheat flour and cut off 60 g pieces. Make rolls and glaze with water. Dip in, e.g. poppy seeds, sesame seeds or strong grated cheese. Place on a greased tray and leave to rise in an unheated oven for 45–60 minutes until doubled in size. Spray with water a few times to prevent the surface from drying out. Baking instructions on p. 63.

Classic French Rolls

Divide the dough into four pieces and make tight balls. Cover with a tea-towel and leave for 10 minutes. Make loaves (see instructions on p. 35). These can be plain or glazed with water and dipped in poppy seeds, sesame seeds or cheese. Leave to rise until doubled in size as for rolls. Then make four diagonal slashes across the top with a sharp knife. Baking instructions on p. 63.

6-strand French Bread

Divide the dough in half, cut off 12 125 g pieces and make oblong rolls. Cover with a tea-towel and leave for 5 minutes. Roll out into long strands, see picture 1, and make a firm plait. Glaze with water and sprinkle with poppy seeds or leave as they are. Leave to rise until doubled in size as for rolls. Baking instructions on p. 63.

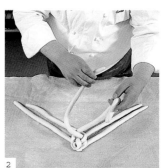

1   2   3   4

Royal Bread

Soak 100 g of raisins in cold water for 30 minutes. Drain, pat dry and mix into the dough. Cut off 400 g pieces and shape into long strands. Make a coil, placing the seam on the bottom of the bread and press to seal. Glaze with water and sprinkle with poppy seeds. Leave to rise as for rolls. Baking instructions on p. 63.

Knots

Roll out the dough, cut off 60 g pieces and shape like hot dog bread. Cover with a tea-towel and leave for 5 minutes. Roll out as in the picture below or to the right, pinch off a third, make a plait and turn over seam down. Glaze with water and sprinkle with poppy seeds. Leave to rise as for rolls. Baking instructions on p. 63.

Lips

Roll out the dough and shape into 60 g balls. Cover and leave for 5 minutes. Roll two at a time with a rolling pin to make "lips". Fold over, glaze with water and dip in poppy seeds. Leave to rise as for rolls. Baking instructions on p. 63.

Large knot

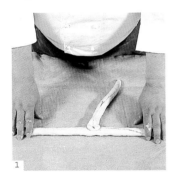

Small knot

Semmeln

Make 60 g rolls and leave for 5 minutes covered by a tea-towel. Make the rolls slightly oblong and leave to rise until doubled in size. Cut a diagonal slash and continue to rise. Baking instructions on p. 63

Schlumbergeli

In Switzerland they make Schlumbergerli from the same dough omitting the egg and 50 g flour for a lighter result. The rolls should be very well baked.

Roll out the dough and cut off 60 g pieces. Brush the work surface with 2 tbsp olive oil and make the bread on this surface to prevent them from getting sticky underneath. The oil makes them crack a little. Sprinkle wheat flour on a tea-towel and turn the floured side up during baking. Baking instructions on p. 63.

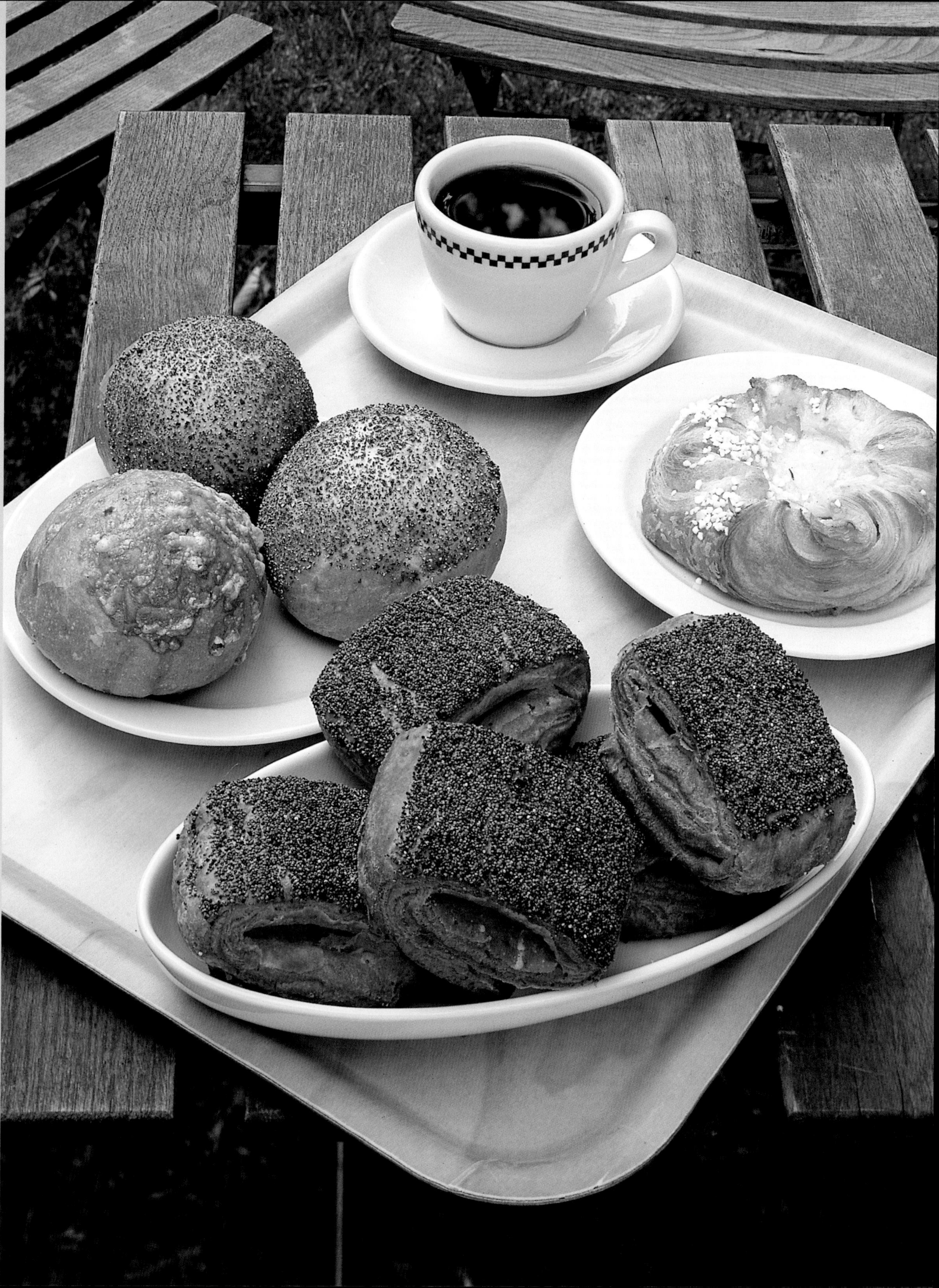

Rolls (p. 60), Tebirkes (p. 194) and Danish Pastries (p. 192).

Crescents

Make round balls with 60 g pieces of dough and leave under a tea-towel for 5 minutes. Use a little wheat flour to roll them out, two at a time, in the form of 1 mm thick "tongues". Make taut crescent shapes by pulling the dough back and forth, see below. Brush with water and dip in poppy seeds. Bend slightly and place on a tray. Leave to rise like rolls.

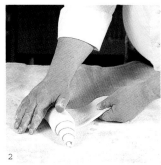

1   2

BAKNING

1. After the bread and rolls have doubled in size, take them out and preheat the oven to 230°C.
2. Place the loaves or rolls in the oven and spray generously with water.
3. Lower the temperature to 200°C after 5 minutes. After another 10 minutes, open the oven door to let in some air. Repeat twice during baking.
4. The 60 g rolls should be baked for 18–20 minutes, loaves for approx. 30–35 minutes and the 6-strand plait and the royal bread for approx. 40 minutes. The thin crescents are quicker, they take about 12 minutes.

Spray the bread with water immediately after thay have been removed from the oven for a nice, crackled surface, which is characteristic of good French bread.

Rolls.

1. French loaves.   2. French rolls.   3. Various French breads.   4. Schlumbergeli.

Zopf

This soft, delicious Sunday bread is a Swiss specialty. You eat it on Sunday morning cut into thick slices with butter and strawberry jam.

Plaited loaves have a different texture from solid bread. They are also better at retaining moisture and therefore keep fresh longer. (Pictures on pp. 66, 56).

2 loaves
Ideal dough temperature 26°C.

20 g yeast	75 g butter
10 g set honey	8 g salt
250 g full-fat milk (2.5 dl)	
750 g strong wheat flour, preferably stone ground	1 egg and a pinch of salt for glazing.
75 g sugar	
100 g egg (2 eggs)	

STARTER

Mix yeast, honey and milk. Pour 250 g of the flour into a bowl, add the yeast mixture and whisk until smooth. Cover with cling-film and leave for 30 minutes.

KNEADING

1. Add the remaining flour, sugar and egg. Knead for 3 minutes on the lowest speed.
2. Add butter and work the dough for another 5 minutes. Add the salt, increase the speed and knead for 10 minutes until it is very elastic and firm. Test for elasticity.
3. Place the dough in a lightly oiled lidded plastic container and leave for 30 minutes.
4. Turn it out on a floured work surface and divide into four equal parts. Make 4 taut balls of dough and cover with a tea-towel leave for 5 minutes.

5. Roll the balls into strands with slightly tapering ends and place them as in the picture below. Cross your arms to make a plait. Press down the ends to seal. Place the loaves on a baking tray.
6. Whisk an egg with a pinch of salt and glaze the loaves.
7. Leave to rise for 60–75 minutes until doubled in size.
8. Preheat the oven to 220°C and glaze the loaves again.
9. Lower the heat to 190°C after 5 minutes. Bake for approx. 35 minutes.
10. Take the tray out of the oven and leave the bread to cool on a wire rack.

You can easily get addicted to Zopf. The bread freezes well in plastic bags and is very nice to toast.

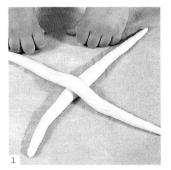

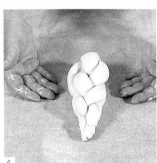

Zopf (p. 65).

White Bread with Levain

This old-fashioned, classic basic dough gives a very well-flavoured bread with a wonderful interior and chewy crust. No other bread goes better with food. Rolls or baguettes made with this basic dough are equally good. Consult p. 30, Baking with Levain, before you start. (Pictures on pp. 68–71).

4 loaves
Ideal dough temperature 26ºC.

1,000 g strong wheat flour,	630 g water (6.3 dl)
preferably stone-ground	20 g sea salt
800 g levain, see p. 30	

1. Pour all the ingredients, except salt, into the mixing bowl. Knead the dough on low speed for 13 minutes, add the salt, increase the speed and knead for 7 minutes until the dough is very elastic. Test for elasticity.
2. Place the dough in a lightly oiled lidded plastic container and leave for 170 minutes.
3. I have made a number of different types of bread from this basic recipe. When making the loaves you place the dough on a work surface sprinkled with flour and divide it into four equal parts. Dust four rectangular baskets with plenty of flour. Fold the loaves over gently and place them in the baskets seam down.
4. Sprinkle flour over them, cover with a tea-towel and leave to rise at room temperature for 75 minutes until doubled in size. If you are not using baskets pull up the cloth up between the loaves and leave to rise the same way. Leaving them in the fridge until the next day gives the best result.
5. Preheat the oven with the stone or tray to 250ºC.
6. Gently turn out the loaves and place them seam up in the oven. Spray generously with water.
7. Lower the temperature to 200ºC after 5 minutes. After another 10 minutes, open the oven door to let in some air. Repeat twice during baking.
8. Bake for 50 minutes, the bread should be rather dark with a hard crust.
9. Take the bread out of the oven, place on a wire rack and spray with water so they crack up.

La couronne bordelaise

This is a beautiful, classic bread made from the same dough as White Bread with Levain.

3 loaves

1 batch White Bread with Levain.

Make the dough and follow the instructions for White Bread with Levain.

1. Divide the dough into three. Cut off three pieces, one from each piece of dough, and shape into a ball.
2. Triple-fold the remaining pieces and cover with a tea-towel.
3. Roll out the small dough balls thinly using a little wheat flour. Sift wheat flour into round baskets with a bulge in the centre. Place the thin pieces of dough over the bulge and press down.
4. Roll out the pieces of dough and cut each length into eight equal parts. Make rolls and place eight in each basket seam down. Dust with wheat flour, cover with a tea-towel and leave to rise as for White Bread with Levain. If you are not using baskets you can do as I have done at the top of the picture on p. 71. I have placed eight rolls in a circle on the baking tray, dusted them with flour and left them to rise under cover. If you are using baskets you should turn the loaves on the tray. Slash the rolls and the wreath before baking and bake as for White Bread with Levain, but only for 35 minutes.

This bread freezes well in plastic bags and should be defrosted in the oven.

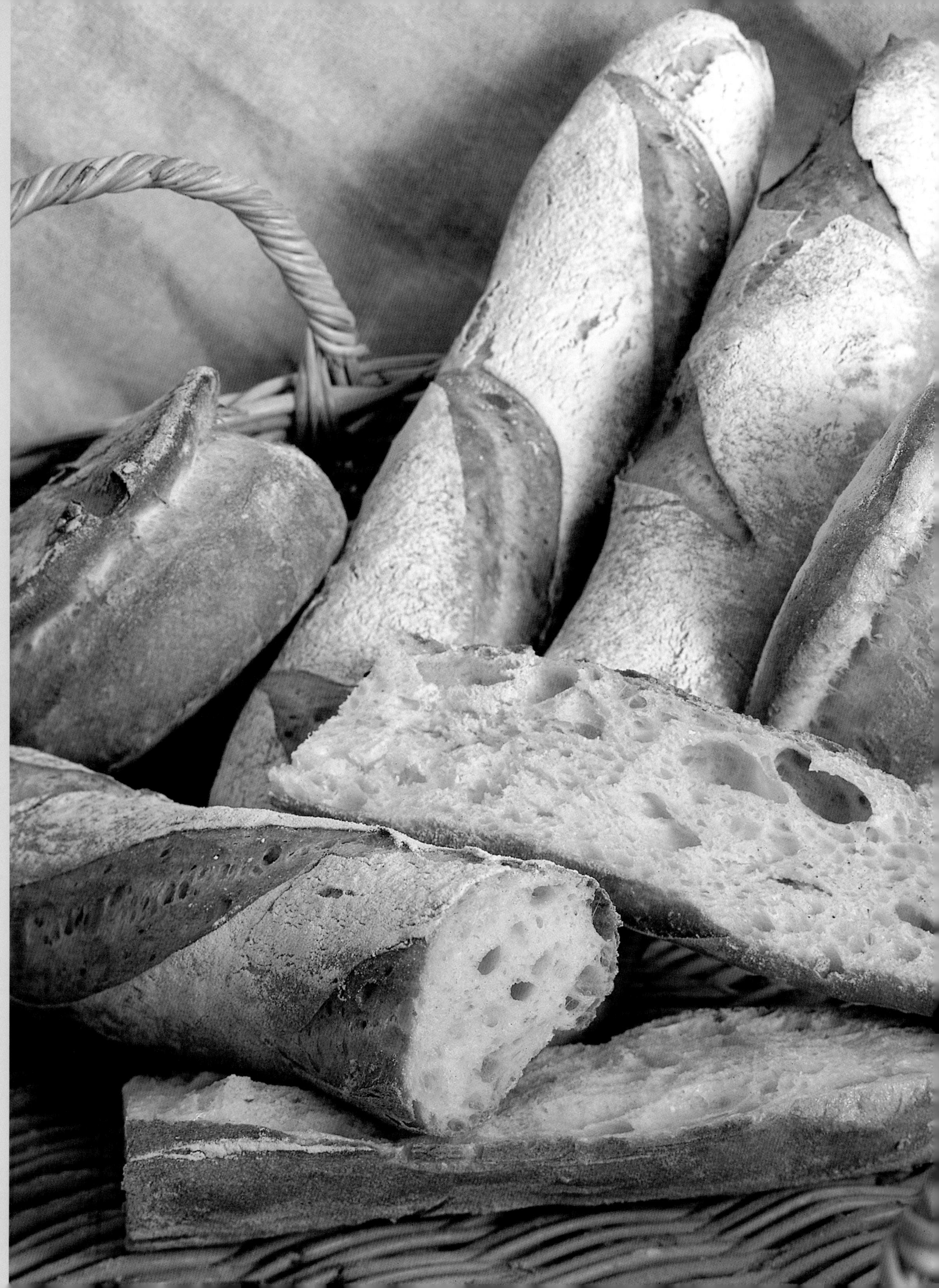

White Bread with Levain (p. 67).

White Bread with Levain (p. 67).

La couronne bordelaise (p. 67).

WHOLEMEAL BREAD

Sourdough Bread with Rye Flour

This is one of my favourites. It has a crisp crust and a soft, well-flavoured, tangy interior. It reminds of the Russian bread we bought in Saint Petersburg to serve with caviare when I used to work on cruise liners. (See picture on p. 75)

2 loaves
Ideal dough temperature 24°C .

DAY 1	DAY 2
POOLISH	KNEADING
3 g yeast	10 g yeast
250 g water (2.5 dl)	250 g water (2.5 dl)
250 g fine rye flour	600 g strong wheat flour
	250 g sourdough made with rye flour (p. 29)
	10 g honey
	20 g sea salt
	20 g havssalt

DAY 1

Make a polish by dissolving the yeast in the water, add flour and whisk until smooth. Cover with cling-film and leave to rise for 24 hours at room temperature.

DAY 2

KNEADING

1. Dissolve the yeast in the water, pour over the wheat flour and add the sourdough, poolish and honey. Knead on the lowest speed for 11 minutes.
2. Add salt and knead for another 5–6 minutes. Make sure you do not work the dough for too long.
3. Place the dough in a lightly oiled plastic container with a lid and leave for 120 minutes. Knock back the dough after half the time.
4. Place on a work top dusted with flour and divide in half. Shape the bread gently into loaves without squeezing out the air. Dust rectangular baskets with rye flour and place the loaves seam down. Sprinkle with rye flour. Cover with a tea-towel and leave to rise for 75 minutes until doubled in size.
5. Preheat the oven with the stone or tray to 250°C.
6. Place the loaves in the oven and spray them generously with water.
7. Lower the heat to 200°C after 5 minutes. Open the oven door to let some air in after another 10 minutes. Repeat twice during baking for a good crust.
8. Bake for a total of 60 minutes. Take out the bread and cool on a wire rack.

Suitable for freezing in plastic bags. Defrost in the oven before serving.

Fig Bread

This rye bread with the added sweetness of figs is particularly delicious with cheese and prosciutto.

2 loaves

1 batch Sourdough Bread made with rye flour

300 g dried figs
100 g pistachios

Mix and prepare the dough as for Sourdough Bread dough made with rye flour.

1. Dice the figs and soak them for 30 minutes in 1 l of cold water. Drain.
2. Dice the figs and pistachios into the dough. Leave as for Sourdough bread made with rye flour, point 3.
3. Place the dough on a floured surface. Divide it into six round balls. Dust two rectangular baskets with coarse rye flour and place three balls in each, seam down.
4. Dust with rye flour and cover with a tea-towel. Leave to rise for approx. 75 minutes until double in size. Bake as for the above bread and leave to cool on a wire rack.

Top left, Fig Bread (p. 74); bottom left, Bread from Tirol (p. 78); top right Sourdough Bread with Rye Flour (p. 74); bottom right Bread from Basel (p. 78).

Sunflower Seed Bread

I love the smell of freshly roasted sunflower seeds. Because of its shape, I call this Turban Bread. (See opposite page)

4 loaves
Ideal dough temperature 26°C.

DAY 1
POOLISH
5 g yeast
250 g water (2.5 dl)
250 g fine rye flour

DAY 2
KNEADING
Kneading
15 g yeast
250 g water 2.5 dl)
25 g set honey
150 g wholemeal flour
500 g strong wheat flour,
    preferably stone ground
50 g sunflower oil
20 g sea salt

DAY 1
POOLISH
Whisk together yeast, water and flour to a smooth batter. Cover with cling film and leave to rise at room temperature for at least 8–15 hours or overnight.

DAY 2
KNEADING
Preheat the oven to 200°C and toast the sunflower seeds on a tray for approx. 10 minutes.

1. Dissolve the yeast, add poolish, honey and flour and knead the dough on low speed for 3 minutes. Add the oil and knead for another 10 minutes. Add salt, increase the speed and knead for another 5 minutes. Test for elasticity. Do not work too long since the dough contains wholemeal flour.
2. Add sunflower seeds and place in a lightly oiled plastic container with a lid. Leave for 90 minutes. Knock back at least once after half the time.
3. Place on a floured work surface and divide into four + one 100 g pieces. Make small rolls. Divide the 100 g piece into four and form small rolls.
4. Cover with a tea-towel and leave for 10 minutes.
5. Press hard with the rolling pin to form eight segments, stick the small bread roll in the middle. Brush with water and sprinkle with sunflower seeds.
6. Dust two tea-towels with flour and place the four loaves on them. Cover with a cloth and leave to rise for approx. 60–75 minutes until doubled in size.
7. Preheat the oven with the stone or tray to 250°C .
8. Put two of the loaves in the oven and spray generously with water. Meanwhile, place the other two in the fridge until the rest are done.
9. Lower the temperature to 200°C after 5 minutes. After another 10 minutes, open the oven door to let in some air. Repeat twice during baking for a crisper crust.
10. Bake for a total of 40 minutes.
11. Take out the loaves and cool on a wire rack. Spray with water for a nicely crackled crust.

Suitable for freezing in plastic bags.

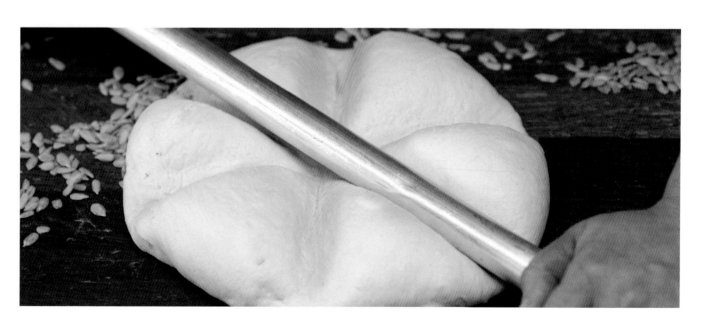

Bread from the Tirol

This bread evokes the contryside in Austria and Germany, a good sausage, cheese and a cold beer. (See picture on p. 75).

2 loaves
Ideal dough temperature 26°C.

DAG 1	**DAG 2**
STARTER	KNEADING
200 g water (2 dl)	20 g yeast
50 g sourdough made with	400 g water (4 dl)
rye flour, see p. 29	260 g fine rye flour,
360 g fine rye flour,	preferably stone ground
preferably stone ground	260 g strong wheat flour
	10 g whole caraway seeds
	20 g sea salt

DAG 1

STARTER

Mix all the ingredients and knead for 10 minutes. Place the dough in a lightly oiled plastic container with a lid and leave for at least 12 hours at room temperature.

DAG 2

KNEADING

1. Dissolve the yeast in the water and add the starter. Add flour and caraway seeds. Knead on the lowest speed for 10 minutes. Add salt and work for 7 min.
2. Place in a lightly oiled plastic container with a lid and leave for 60 minutes, knock back once.
3. Place the dough on a floured work surface, divide it in two and make two round balls. Place these on a tea-towel dusted with flour, cover and leave to rise for 30 minutes. Make an indentation at the centre with a rolling pin and leave to rise for 30 minutes.
4. Preheat the oven with the stone or tray to 250°C.
5. Place the bread in the oven using a large spatula and spray generously with water.
6. Lower the temperature to 200°C after 5 minutes. After another 10 minutes, open the oven door to let some air in. Repeat twice during baking.
7. Bake for a total of 40 minutes. Take out the bread, place them on a wire rack and spray with water.

Tip
This moist bread keep fresh for a whole week, but they are also suitable for freezing.

Bread from Basel

This dark, crusty bread with a hard crust always come in pairs. The crust is crisp with a distinct taste of roasted flour and the inside is fluffy and moist due to the loose dough. The dough must be knocked back at least twice in order to keep its shape. This is one of my favourite breads. (See picture on p. 75).

2 loaves
Ideal dough temperature 24°C.

STARTER	KNEADING
5 g yeast	15 g yeast
250 g water (2.5 dl)	250 g water (2.5 dl)
200 g fine rye flour, 50 g	450 g strong wheat flour,
sourdough made with rye	preferably stone ground
flour	18 g sea salt

STARTER

Dissolve the yeast in the water and pour over the rye flour and sourdough. Knead on the lowest speed for 10 minutes. Place in a lightly oiled plastic container with a lid and leave to rise at room temperature for 3 hours.

KNEADING

1. Dissolve the yeast in the water and pour it over the starter. Add wheat flour. Knead the dough on the lowest speed for 10 minutes. Add the salt and work for another 9 minutes on a higher speed. The dough should be very elastic. Make the elasticity test.
2. Place the dough in a lightly oiled plastic container with a lid and leave for 120 minutes, knock back the dough three times during rising.
3. Place on a floured work surface, divide it into four pieces. Gently roll into small oblong shapes.
4. Dust two rectangular baskets generously with rye flour. Place the loaves inside, two at a time seam down. Dust with flour and cover. Leave to rise for approx. 60 minutes until doubled in size.
5. Preheat the oven with the stone or tray to 275°C.
6. Place the bread in the oven and spray generously with water.
7. Lower the temperature to 200°C after 5 minutes. After another 10 minutes open the oven door and let some air in. Repeat twice during baking.
8. Bake for a total of 50 minutes for a dark and crusty bread.

9. Take out the bread and cool on a wire rack. Spray with water for a nicely crackled surface.

Freeze well in plastic bags. When heated up in the oven they taste as good as fresh.

St Gallen Bürlibrot

This delicious bread is a standard lunchtime bread at all Swiss restaurants. It has a typical brittle crust with a thick coat of flour and a fluffy interior. The dinkel flour gives it a strong, bready flavour and cannot be replaced by any other flour.

2 loaves or 16 rolls
Ideal dough temperature 26°C.

DAY 1	DAY 2
STARTER	KNEADING
1 g yeast	300 g dinkel flour,
100 g water (1 dl)	80 g fine rye flour,
150 g dinkel flour,	preferable stone ground
wholemeal	350 g strong wheat flour
1 g sea salt	100 g sourdough made with
	rye flour, see p. 29
	25 g yeast
	400 g water
	20 g sea salt

STARTER
Dissolve the yeast in the water. Pour over the flour. Knead the dough for 10 minutes on low speed. Add the salt and knead for another 5 minutes. Place the dough in a lightly oiled plastic container with a lid and leave to rise for 12–15 hours or over night at room temperature.

KNEADING
1. Add the starter and sourdough to the flours. Dissolve the rest of the yeast in the water and pour it over the flour mixture.
2. Knead the dough on the lowest speed for 10 minutes and add the salt. Increase the speed and work for another 8 minutes until you get a rather loose and elastic dough.
3. Place it in a lightly oiled plastic container with a lid and leave for 120 minutes. Knock back the dough twice during rising.

LOAVES
4. Divide the dough and make two round balls. Place each in a round basket that has been dusted with dinkel flour. Cover with a towel and leave to rise for 45 minutes until doubled in size.
5. Preheat the oven with the stone or tray to 250°C.
6. Place the bread in the oven and spray generously with water.
7. Lower the temperature to 200°C after 5 minutes. After another 10 minutes, open the oven door to let the air in. Repeat twice during baking for a crisper crust.
8. Bake for a total of 50 minutes.
9. Take out the bread, place them on a wire rack and spray with water for a nice, crackled crust.

ROLLS
4. Roll out the dough and cut off 80 g pieces. Shape rolls on the oiled surface. Sprinkle fine rye flour over the tea-towel and place the rolls two and two seam down. Leave to rise until double in size.
5. Turn the rolls over with the seam facing up. Bake as for loaves, reducing the baking time to 26 min.

Suitable for freezing in plastic bags.

Fougnole des Pyrénées with Levain

When I make this well-flavoured bread I mix the wild yeast from the levain with regular yeast. When you are baking with levain, you need to plan well ahead, see p.30. It is well worth it, however – the result is wonderful.

I got this recipe years ago on a course in traditional French bread making at the Lenôtre school in Paris.

2 loaves
Ideal dough temperature 26 °C.

KNEADING
25 g yeast
500 g water (5 dl)
200 g fine rye flour,
    preferably stone ground

575 g strong wheat flour,
    preferably stone ground
350 g levain, see p. 31
18 g salt

KNEADING

1. Dissolve the yeast in the water. Pour the mixture over the flour mixture, add levain and knead for 13 minutes on the lowest speed. Add the salt, increase the speed and work for another 7 minutes. Test for elasticity.
2. Place the dough in a lightly oiled plastic container with a lid and leave for 60 minutes. Knock back the dough after half the time.
3. Turn it out on a floured work surface and divide into two. Make two tight balls.
4. Cover with a tea-towel and leave for 10 minutes.
5. Roll out 1/3 of one of the dough balls (5 mm thick) using wheat flour, fold the thin part over the thick and press together with a rolling pin, see picture on p. 49. Repeat with the remaining ball. Place the two loaves on a tea-towel dusted with flour and leave to rise until doubled in size, approx. 60 minutes.
6. Preheat the oven with the stone or tray to 250ºC.
7. Place the bread in the oven and spray them with water.
8. Lower the temperature to 200 ºC after 5 minutes. After another 10 minutes, open the oven door to let the air in. Repeat twice during baking.
9. Bake for a total of 50 minutes.
10. Place on a wire rack and spray with water for a nice, crackled crust.

Raisin and Hazelnut Loaf

This delicious breakfast bread keeps for days thanks to the raisins. It goes very well with cheese.

For a number of years I worked as a consultant to an American raisin producer in California, and I learned a lot about raisins in their test bakery. Remember always to soak them in cold water before using. Otherwise they will soak up the moisture in the bread and make it dry.

To make the bread rise quicker you can add 3 g yeast to the dough, but the result is not quite as good. See Baking with Levain on p. 30, before you begin. See picture on p. 81.

2 large loaves
Ideal dough temperature is 26ºC.

250 g California raisins
300 g Italian or Spanish hazelnuts

500 g water (5 dl)
400 g levain, see p. 31
500 g fine rye flour,
preferably stone ground

300 g strong wheat flour,
    preferably stone ground
50 g set honey
18 g sea salt

1. Soak the raisins for 30 minutes in plenty of cold water. Drain in a sieve. Preheat the oven to 200ºC. Roast the hazelnuts on a tray until they are golden brown and the skins are starting to peel, approx. 10 minutes. Rub off the skins using a towel and remove.
2. Pour the rest of the ingredients, except the salt, into the mixing bowl. Knead on the lowest speed for 10 minutes. Add the salt and knead on low speed for another 5 minutes.
3. Add the drained raisins and the coarsely chopped hazelnuts.
4. Place the dough in a lightly oiled plastic container with a lid and leave for 120 minutes. Knock back the dough twice during rising.
5. Turn out on a floured work surface, fold and pull the dough to shape long, slightly tapered loaves.
6. Place on a tea-towel dusted with flour and sprinkle with fine rye flour. Cover and leave to rise for about 120 minutes until doubled in size.
7. Preheat the oven with the stone or tray to 250ºC.

8. Place the loaves in the oven and spray generously with water.

9. Lower the heat to 200ºC after 5 minutes. After another 10 minutes, open the oven door to let the air in. Repeat twice during baking for a drier heat.

10. Bake for 50 minutes. Use a thermometer to check when the bread is ready (98ºC) since the moist raisins require longer baking times.

11. Take out the bread and cool on a wire rack.

This bread is suitable for freezing in plastic bags.

Left, Raisin and Hazelnut Bread with Levain; right, Pause Bread.

Classic French Farmer's Loaf with Levain.

Classic French Farmer's Loaf

This delicious and crusty bread is called Pain de Campagne in French. Due to the long rising time the bread is light and fluffy with a thick crust and well-flavoured interior. Leaving it to rise in a cold place overnight improves the aroma and texture. It goes well with all good food and cheese. You can add 3 g of yeast if you like, but it tastes better without it. See Baking with Levain, p. 30, before you begin. (See opposite).

2 large loaves
Ideal dough temperature 26°C.

500 g water (5dl)	650 g strong wheat flour
400 g levain, see p. 31	18 g sea salt
75 g wholemeal flour, preferably stone ground	
50 g fine rye flour, preferably stone ground	

1. Pour all the ingredients except the salt into the mixing bowl and knead on the lowest speed for 13 minutes. Add the salt, increase the speed and work until very elastic for another 5 minutes. Test for elasticity.
2. Place the dough in a lightly oiled plastic container with a lid and leave for 120 minutes, knock back the dough twice during rising.
3. Turn out on a floured work surface and cut in two. Make two tight balls of dough, place them on a towel dusted with flour and sprinkle with wholemeal flour. Cover with another towel.
4. Leave to rise until doubled in size for approx. 120 minutes or in the fridge overnight for an even better aroma.
5. Preheat the oven with the stone or tray to 250°C.
6. Slash the loaves with a sharp knife or razor blade.
7. Place in the oven and spray generously with water.
8. Lower the temperature to 200°C after 5 minutes. After another 10 minutes, open the oven door to let the air in. Repeat twice during baking.
9. Bake for 60 minutes
10. Take out the bread, place on a wire rack and spray with water for a crackled crust.

Pain de campagne traditionnel

Below is a variation of Classic French Farmer's Loaf with Levain, but the procedure is the same. Try both and see which one you like best.

2 loaves
Ideal dough temperature 26°C.

500 g water (5 dl)	80 g fine rye flour,
400 g levain, see p. 31	preferably stone ground
700 g strong wheat flour, preferably stone ground	18 g sea salt

1. Pour all the ingredients except the salt into the mixing bowl and knead on the lowest speed for 13 minutes. Add the salt, increase the speed and work until very elastic for another 5 minutes. Test for elasticity.
2. Place the dough in a lightly oiled plastic container with a lid and leave for 120 minutes, knock back the dough twice during rising.
3. Turn out on a floured work surface and cut in two. Make two tight balls of dough, place them on a towel dusted with flour and sift rye flour over them. Cover with another towel.
4. Leave to rise until doubled in size for approx. 120 minutes or in the fridge overnight for an even better aroma.
5. Turn on the oven at 250°C with the stone or tray in place.
6. Slash the loaves with a sharp knife or razor blade.
7. Place the bread in the oven and spray generously with water.
8. Lower the temperature to 200°C after 5 minutes. After another 10 minutes, open the oven door to let the air in. Repeat twice during baking.
9. Bake for 60 minutes
10. Take out the loaves, place on a wire rack and spray with water for a crackled crust.

Pain de campagne rustique

This bread is slightly more rustic than the Pain de Campagne Traditionnel, hence the name. It goes well with country food. Read Baking with Levain, p. 30, before you begin. (See picture opposite)

2 loaves
Ideal dough temperature 28°C

500 g water (5dl)
400 g levain, see p. 31
400 g strong wheat flour,
   preferably stone ground

150 g wholemeal flour
20 g sea salt

Follow the instructions for Classic French Farmer's Loaf with Levain, p. 83
1. Turn out on a floured work surface and cut in two.
2. Make two tight balls of dough, place them seam up in two baskets generously dusted with flour. Cover with another towel.
3. Leave to rise until doubled in size for approx. 120 minutes.
4. Preheat the oven with the stone or tray to 250°C.
5. Turn the loaves with a spatula and slash an X across the top with a sharp knife. Place the them in the oven and spray generously with water.
6. Lower the temperature to 200°C after 5 minutes. After another 10 minutes, open the oven door to let the air in. Repeat twice during baking.
7. Bake for 60 minutes
8. Take out the bread and place on a wire rack.

Suitable for freezing in plastic bags.

Le pain de Lodève

This crusty bread has a wonderful flavour. It should be full of large holes, dark in colour and have a crisp crust. The dough contains levain, so take a look at p. 30, Baking with Levain, before you begin.

When I studied in Basel I met a Frenchman who owned a small patisserie and bakery outside Strasbourg. This bread was his speciality, and there were always a queue of people who wanted to buy them.

4 loaves

500 g strong wheat flour,
   preferably stone ground
500 g wholemeal dinkel
   flour

800 g levain, see p. 31
730 g water (7.3 dl)
25 g sea salt

Mix the dough according to the recipe for White Bread with Levain on p. 67.
1. Place the dough in a plastic container greased with olive oil, close the lid and leave for 170 minutes, knock back the dough twice during rising.
2. Turn out the loose dough on a work surface lightly greased with olive oil and then dusted with flour.
3. Preheat the oven with the stone or tray to 250°C.
4. Dust the dough with wheat flour. Make four square loaves.
5. Place the loaves in the oven and spray carefully with water.
6. Lower the temperature to 200°C after 5 minutes. After another 10 minutes, open the oven door to let the air in. Repeat twice during baking.
7. Bake for 45 minutes.
8. Take out the loaves and leave to cool on a wire rack.

Pain de campagne rustique (p. 84).

Baguette and Farmer's Loaf

This delicious baguette works well as a wholemeal alternative to sandwich bread with a seafood topping. Consult p. 30, Baking with Levain, before you begin.

Approx. 5 loaves
Ideal dough temperature 24°C.

100 g toasted sesame seeds	50 g dark muscovado sugar
600 g strong wheat flour, preferably stone ground	20 g yeast
150 g wholemeal flour preferably stone ground	670 g (6.7 dl)
	25 g sea salt

800 g levain

1. Turn on the oven at 200°C, place the sesame seeds on a baking tray and toast for approx. 10 minutes. Cool.
2. Put all the ingredients except salt and sesame seeds in a mixing bowl. Knead the dough on the lowest speed for 13 minutes. Add the salt and increase the speed. Work for 5 minutes until the dough is elastic. Do not work too long. Add the cold sesame seeds towards the end.
3. Place the dough in an oiled plastic container with a lid and leave for 170 minutes.

BAGUETTES

1. Divide into 350 g pieces, fold in three and leave for 15 minutes. Roll out baguettes with tapered ends the length of the baking tray. Place the baguettes on a tea-towel dusted with flour and pull up the cloth between each bread. Dust with flour and cover.
2. Leave to rise for approx. 120 minutes until doubled in size.
3. Preheat the oven with the stone or tray to 240 °C.
4. Take out a ruler or wooden plank that is twice as wide and the same length as the baguettes. Roll them one at a time onto the plank and make three diagonal slashes. Bake three at a time. Spray generously with water.
5. Lower the temperature to 200°C after 5 minutes. After another 10 minutes, open the oven door to let the air in.
6. Take out the baguettes after 30 minutes, place on a wire rack and spray with water for an attractively crackled surface.

LOAVES

Divide the dough into four. Make round, tight buns and place them on a floured tea-towel. Sprinkle with wholemeal flour and leave to rise as for baguettes. Slash a pattern across the top as in the picture and bake two at a time, keeping the other two in the fridge. Bake for 45 minutes and cool on a wire rack.

These freeze well in plastic bags. Remove the bag before defrosting at room temperature or in the oven.

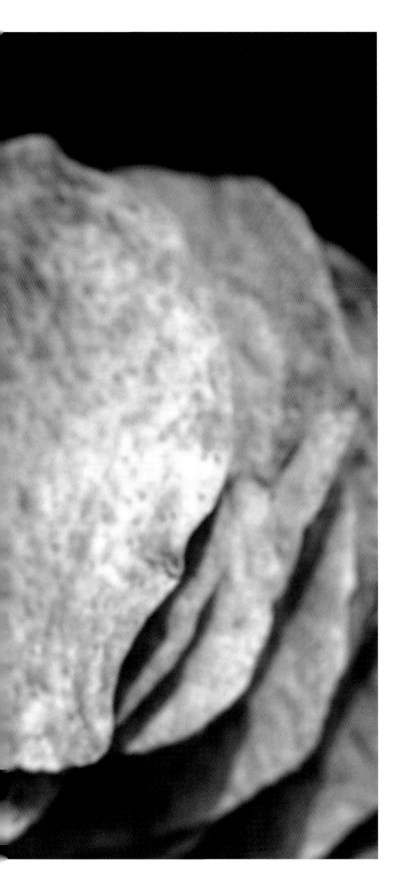

Crisp Bread

This recipe is courtesy of Erik Olofson of Rosendal in Stockholm.

approx. 8 round cakes

STARTER	KNEADING
15 g yeast	100 g coarse rye flour
500 g full-fat milk (5 dl)	200 g strong wheat flour
200 g set honey	10 g sea salt
100 g rye sourdough, p. 29	
700 g wholemeal flour	
150 g coarse rye flour	

STARTER

Dissolve the yeast in the milk and add the honey. Mix with the sourdough and flour to make a smooth batter. Leave to rise covered by cling film for 30–60 minutes.

KNEADING

1. Add rye flour and wheat flour to the starter and knead the dough for 13 minutes on the lowest speed. Add the salt and work the dough for another 2 minutes.
2. Leave for 30 minutes in a lightly oiled lidded plastic container.
3. Turn out on a floured work surface and break off 150 g pieces. Make round buns and cover with a tea-towel.
4. Leave for 10 minutes. Roll out round cakes the size of a dinner plate using rye flour and place on baking trays. Prick with a fork. Use a cake cutter to make a hole in the middle.
5. Preheat the oven to 200°C and bake for 14 minutes until golden brown. Leave to cool on a wire rack.

Store in a dry place.

Pumpernickel (p. 100) and Müsli Bread.

Müsli Bread

This is a type of wholemeal bread that dries out easily. To prevent this I have scalded the flour to increase the water content, resulting in a moist, well-flavoured bread. Great with butter and apricot jam. (See picture opposite)

2 loaves
Ideal dough temperature 26ºC.
2 2 l rectangular baking tins.

DAY 1

SCALDING	KNEADING
125 g wholemeal flour	575 g wholemeal flour
250 g water (2.5 dl)	50 g butter
	50 g set honey
DAY 2	250 g full-fat milk (2.5 dl)
50 g raisins	25 g yeast
50 g sunflower seeds	18 g sea salt
50 g pumpkin seeds	
50 g chopped walnuts	25 g butter for the tins

DAY 1

SCALDING

Put the flour in a mixing bowl. Pour the boiling water over the flour and stir until you have a smooth porridge-like mixture. Cover with cling-film and leave at room temperature for 24 hours.

DAY 2

1. Soak the raisins in plenty of cold water for 30 minutes and drain in a sieve.
2. Preheat the oven to 200ºC. Toast the sunflower and pumpkin seeds until golden brown. Cool.

KNEADING

1. Put the scalded flour mixture in the mixing bowl. Weigh flour, butter, honey and the yeast/milk mixture. Knead the dough for 13 minutes on the lowest speed. Add salt and knead on a slightly higher speed for another 7 minutes. Test for elasticity.
2. Work in the raisins, sunflower and pumpkin seeds and walnuts.
3. Place the dough in a lightly oiled lidded plastic container an leave for 60 minutes, knock back the dough once during rising.
4. Turn out on a floured work surface and divide it in two. Shape two long rolls and cut each up into six pieces. Butter two 2 l baking tins, shape the dough pieces into oblong rolls and place them side by side in the tins. Glaze lightly with water and sprinkle with oatmeal.
5. Cover with a tea-towel and put the tins in the unheated oven. Leave to rise until doubled in size. Remove the bread from the oven.
6. Preheat the oven to 250ºC. Return the bread to the oven and spray them generously with water.
7. Lower the heat to 180ºC after 5 minutes.
8. Bake for approx. 40 minutes. Use a thermometer to check if the bread is ready (98ºC).
9. Take out the loaves, remove the tins and put the bread back in the oven for another 5 minutes for an even crust all round.

Suitable for freezing and good for toasting.

DARK BREAD

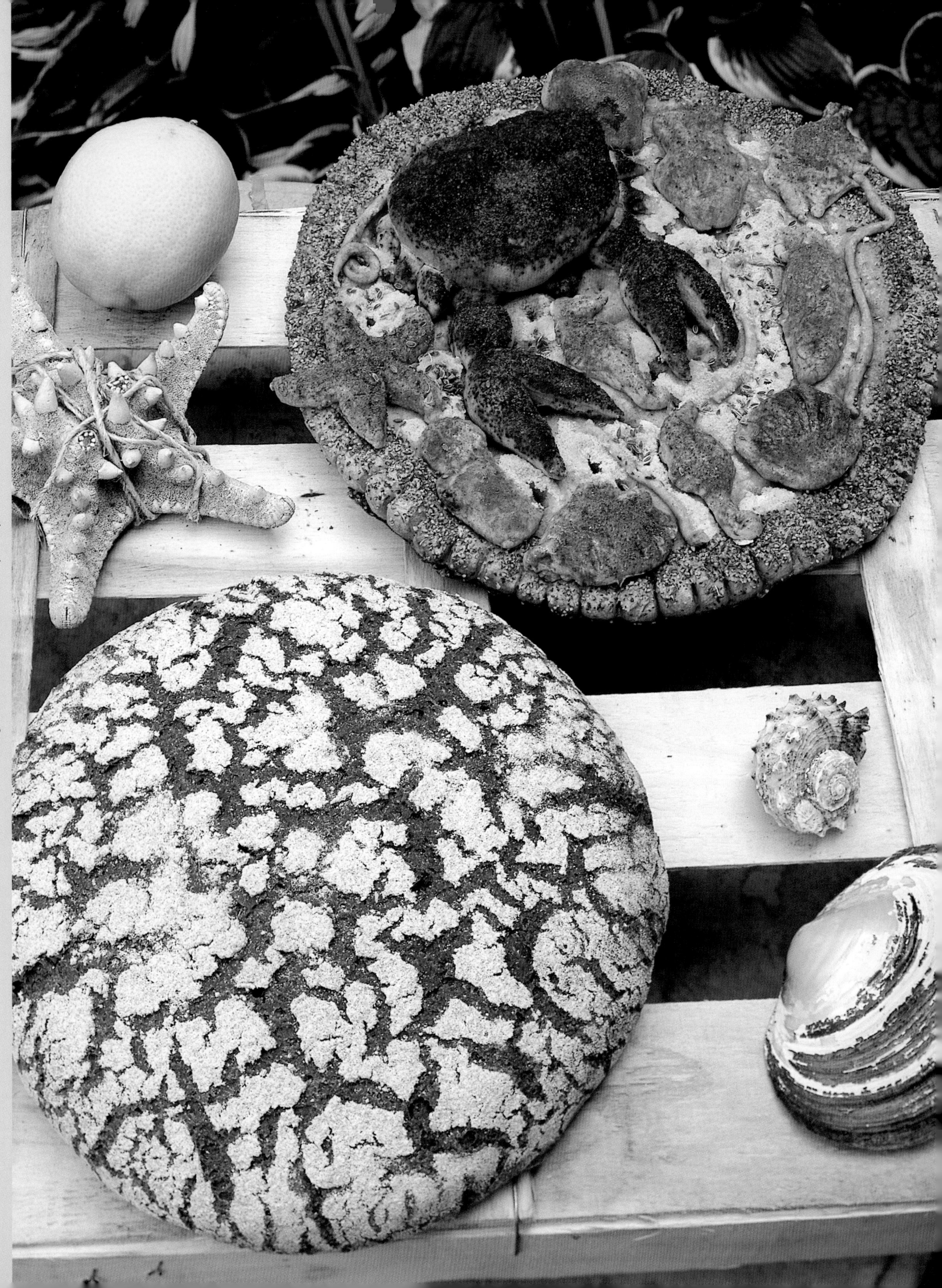

Finnish Rye Bread and Decorative Bread (P. 218).

Finnish Rye Bread

The delicious bread in this recipe was created for Östen Brolin at the Vetekatten bakery in Stockholm. He once told me about his childhood in the north of Sweden and how he longed for the tangy bread that is typical for that region. (See opposite page, bottom)

The Ekberg bakery makes a marvellous rye bread and is well worth a visit if you should find yourself in Helsinki.

2 loaves
Ideal dough temperature 28°C.

DAY 1

STARTER

250 g water, 35°C (2.5 dl)
125 g sourdough with rye flour, mature and active, see p. 29
400 g fine rye flour, preferably stone ground

DAY 2

KNEADING

30 g yeast
180 g water, 35°C (1.8 dl)
500 g buttermilk (5 dl)
675 g fine rye flour
30 g sea salt

DAY 1

STARTER

Beat water, sourdough and rye flour into a thick batter using a whisk and a 4 l mixing bowl. Cover with cling-film and place in an unheated oven or some other place with an even temperature. Leave to rise for at last 12 hours or over night until it is fully mature.

DAY 2

KNEADING

1. Dissolve the yeast in the water and add all the ingredients except the salt. Add the starter and knead on the lowest speed for 10 minutes. Add the salt and knead for another 5 minutes on the lowest speed. The ideal dough temperature is 28°C, which improves rising properties and gives a nicely crackled surface.
2. Leave the dough for 60 minutes in a lightly oiled plastic container with a lid.
3. Place the dough on a floured work surface and divide it in two. Sift some rye flour over a tea-towel and shape two round balls.
4. Place these on the towel and sift over a generous amount of rye flour.
5. Leave to rise at room temperature, 60–90 minutes until doubled in size and the dough begins to crack on the surface.
6. Preheat the oven with the stone or tray to 250°C.
7. Place the breads in the oven using a spatula and spray generously with water.
8. Lower the temperature to 190°C after 5 minutes. Open the oven door after another 10 minutes to let some air in. Repeat twice during baking.
9. Bake the breads for approx. 60 minutes or until the temperature in the centre is 98°C.
10. Take out the breads and cool on a wire rack.

These breads keep for a week in an air-tight container. Also suitable for freezing.

Tip
Thin slices go very well with prosciutto ham, other air-cured meats or oysters and other seafood.

"Quality has always been important to me.
If you spend time doing something
you should make certain the quality is high.
If it isn't you might as well not do it at all!"

Dinkel Bread

The botanical name for dinkel is *Triticum spelta*, hence its other name – spelt. At least half of the flour used in dinkel bread must be dinkel. This recipe gives a wonderful crusty bread to enjoy with soup. (Opposite).

2 loaves

DAY 1	DAY 2
STARTER	KNEADING
2 g yeast	260 g dinkel flour
200 g water, 20°C (2 dl)	400 g strong wheat flour,
300 g dinkel flour	preferably stone ground
50 g rye sourdough, p. 29	20 g yeast
	400 g water, 20°C (4 dl)
	25 g salt

DAY 1

STARTER

Whisk together yeast and water. Weigh the flour and sourdough in the mixing bowl and pour over the water. Knead the dough for 10 minutes on the lowest speed. Place in a lightly oiled plastic container with a lid and leave at room temperature over night.

DAY 2

KNEADING

1. Combine the flours in the bowl and add the starter. Dissolve the yeast in the water and pour into the mixing bowl. Knead the dough on the lowest speed for 10 minutes. Add salt and knead for another 5 minutes. Increase the speed and knead the dough for another 3 minutes until very elastic.
2. Place in a lightly oiled plastic container with a lid and leave for 120 minutes. Knock back twice.
3. Divide into two and gently shape two loaves without applying any pressure. Place the loaves into two rectangular proving baskets dusted with wholemeal dinkel flour.
4. Cover with a tea-towel and leave to rise for approx. 45 minutes or until doubled in size.
5. Preheat the oven with the stone or tray to 250°.
6. Use a sharp knife to make a deep slash along the side of the bread (see the bread to the right opposite), and place in the oven.
7. Spray generously with water.
8. Lower the temperature to 200°C after 5 minutes. Open the oven door after another 10 minutes to let some air in. Repeat twice during baking.
9. Bake for a total of 60 minutes. Cool on a wire rack. Spray with water for a nicely crackled crust.

Suitable for freezing in plastic bags.

Dinkel Bread with Levain

A great bread with a compact interior and strong aroma. You need to start in good time when you bake with levain, it is well worth the trouble! See Baking with Levain, p. 30 (picture opposite).

3 loaves
Ideal dough temperature 26°C.

400 g levain	300 g strong wheat flour,
500 g water (5 dl)	preferably stone ground
100 g coarse rye flour,	18 g sea salt
preferably stone ground	
500 g dinkel flour	

1. Knead all the ingredients except the salt on the lowest speed for 10 minutes. Add the salt, increase speed and work for 7–8 minutes until elastic. Check the texture.
2. Place the dough in lightly oiled plastic container with a lid and leave for 170 minutes.
3. Turn out on a floured work surface and divide it into four equal pieces. Make three round balls and fold the fourth. Cover with a tea-towel and leave for 10 minutes.
4. Form the balls into three loaves. Make a 1 cm thick roll from the remaining piece and cut off 10 g pieces to make small rolls.
5. Sprinkle dinkel flour over the dough and use a rolling pin to make an indentation in the centre. Brush with water and place the rolls next to each other (see picture on p. 98).
6. Sprinkle with dinkel flour and place on a floured tea-towel. Pull up the cloth between the breads so they rise upwards. Cover with a towel and leave to rise until doubled in size for approx. 90 minutes.

Continued on p. 98.

Top left, Rye Bread with Levain (p. 101); right, Dinkel Bread; bottom, Dinkel Bread with Levain.

7. Preheat the oven with the stone or tray to 250°C.
8. Place the breads in the oven and spray generously with water.
9. Lower the temperature to 200°C after 5 minutes. Open the oven door after another 10 minutes to let some air in. Repeat twice during baking.
10. Bake the breads for a total of 40 minutes.
11. Cool on a wire rack.

Freeze in plastic bags.

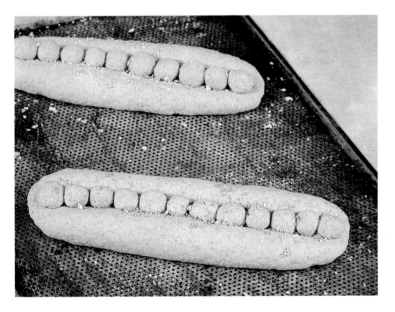

Olof Viktors' Dark Rye Bread

It takes time to make this classic bread from the province of Skåne if you use only rye flour. I created this recipe when we opened the Olof Victors bakery in 2002.

Rye contains no gluten, consequently sourdough must be added to add rising and baking properties causing the pentosanes in the rye to swell, thus trapping the gases in the dough.

To make this bread, you use a little more water at the scalding stage, resulting in a denser bread.

4 loaves
Ideal dough temperature 28°C.

SCALDING
185 g fine rye flour
10 g ground caraway seed
500 g water (5 dl)
40 g sea salt

STARTER
25 g yeast
500 g water
150 g sourdough made with rye flour, see p. 2

KNEADING
20 g yeast
400 g treacle
1 kg fine rye flour or rye/wheat blend

100 g melted butter for glazing

DAY 1
SCALDING
Measure the flour in a mixing bowl and add the ground caraway seed and salt. Boil the water and pour over the mixture and stir using a wooden spoon. Cover with cling-film and leave for 24 hours at room temperature.

DAY 2
STARTER
Dissolve the yeast in the water and sourdough. Add flour and scalded flour. Knead for 5 minutes on low speed. Cover with cling-film and leave to rise for 4 hours.

KNEADING
1. Add the rest of the ingredients and knead for 15 minutes on the lowest speed.
2. Place the dough in a lightly oiled plastic container with a lid and leave for 60 minutes. Turn out on a floured work surface and divide into four.
3. Melt the butter in a small saucepan and set aside.
4. Make rectangular loaves and glaze the sides with melted butter. Brush melted butter on a baking tray and place the breads on it.
5. Cover with a tea-towel and leave to rise for approx. 45 minutes.
6. Preheat the oven to 250°C.
7. Put the breads in the oven and spray generously with water.
8. Lower the temperature to 180°C after 5 minutes. Open the oven door after another 10 minutes to let some air in. Repeat twice during baking.
9. Bake the bread for approx. 90 minutes. Check that the bread is done (98°C).
10. Take out the breads and glaze with melted butter.

This bread freezes well. Defrost on a wire rack at room temperature to avoid moisture forming.

Top, Hard Dark Rye Bread (p. 101); bottom, Olof Viktors' Dark Rye Bread.

Pumpernickel

This is a German specialty from Westphalia. We are accustomed to round, very dark pumpernickel, but there are in fact several varieties. This is a dense and tasty bread with a healthy flavour.

2 loaves
Two 2 l rectangular sponge cake tins.

DAY 1	**DAY 2**
SOAKING	KNEADING
375 g rye kernels	500 g water (5 dl)
375 g water (3.75 dl)	30 g yeast
	700 g coarse rye flour,
STARTER	preferably stone ground
250 g water (2.5 dl)	10 g sea salt
15 g yeast	
310 coarse rye flour	25 g butter for the tins
100 g rye sourdough, p. 29	
2 g salt	

DAY 1
SOAKING
Put the rye kernels in a mixing bowl, heat the water almost to the point of boiling and pour over the kernels, mix with a wooden spoon. Cover with cling-film and leave at room temperature until the next day.

STARTER
Dissolve the water and yeast in a bowl and mix rye flour, sourdough and salt. Knead on the lowest speed for 5 minutes. Place the dough in a lightly oiled plastic container with a lid and leave for a minimum of 12–18 hours at room temperature or in the fridge over night.

DAY 2
KNEADING
1. Pour the water into the mixing bowl and dissolve the yeast. Add the starter and the soaked rye kernels together with rye flour and salt. Knead on low speed for 15 minutes. Place the dough in a lightly oiled plastic container, leave for 30 minutes.
2. Place the dough on a floured work surface and divide into two. Make two loaves and put them in two greased 2 l sponge cake tins. Cover with a towel and leave to rise for 30 minutes.
3. Bake for 5 minutes at 250°C. Reduce the temperature to 170°C and bake for 60 minutes. Check the temperature (98°C).
4. Remove the tray from the oven and cover the tins with a tea-towel. Leave to cool in the tins.

Suitable for freezing in plastic bags.

Whole Grain Bread with Rye Kernels

This healthy and tasty bread with a strong rye flavour goes well with cheese and air-cured meats, but also with strawberry or rhubarb jam. (Picture on p. 102).

2 loaves
Ideal dough temperature 28°C.
Two 2 l rectangular sponge cake tins.

DAY 1	**DAY 2**
SOAKING	KNEADING
500 g water, 90°C (5 dl)	30 g yeast
600 g rye kernels	400 g water (5 dl)
	440 g fine rye flour,
STARTER	preferably stone ground
200 g water (2 dl)	25 g dark honey, e.g.
50 g rye sourdough, p. 29	heather
250 fine rye flour,	24 g sea salt
preferably stone ground	

DAY 1
SOAKING
Heat the water to 90°C, pour it over the rye kernels and mix well with a wooden spoon. Cover with cling-film and leave to swell until the following day. Pour into a sieve and drain. The weight should be approx. 800 g.

STARTER
Mix the ingredients for 10 minutes on the lowest speed. Place the loose dough in a plastic container and leave at room temperature until the next day.

DAY 2
KNEADING
1. Dissolve the yeast in the water and pour it over the rye flour in the mixing bowl. Add the starter, 800 g of the drained kernels, honey and salt and knead on the lowest speed for 15 minutes. Cover with cling-film and leave for 75 minutes.

2. Grease two 2 l sponge cake tins. Pour the dough into the tins and level the surface with a spoon dipped in water. Leave to rise in a warm place for approx. 60 minutes.
3. Preheat the oven with the stone or tray to 250ºC.
4. Place the tins in the oven and spray generously with water.
5. Bake for approx. 60 minutes. Use a thermometer to check that the temperature is 98º.
6. Take out the tins, immediately remove the loaves, put them on a tray and bake for another 5 minutes for a hard crust all over. A soft crust will make the bread go mouldy.
7. Wrap in a towel to cool to avoid the bread from getting too hard.

This delicious bread keeps for weeks in the fridge.

Hard Dark Rye Bread

Hard Dark Rye Bread is a traditional bread from the province of Skåne, and the Mellby bakers make the best. It is also a traditional bread in Germany where it is called Kastenbrot. (See picture on p. 99).

Use the same recipe as for Dark Rye Bread from Olof Viktors, p. 98, but substitute 200 g of the treacle for sourdough based on rye flour and omit the caraway seeds.

Shape the loaves as for Dark Rye Bread from Olof Viktors, p. 98, but place two breads on the tray and press them flat. Glaze with melted butter, put the other on top and press. Leave to rise and bake as for the above bread. When they are baked you break them up, put them back in the oven and turn it off. Leave to dry until the next day.

Thinly sliced, this bread goes very well with smoked sausages or pickled herring.

Rye Bread with Levain

Rye Bread with Levain, or Pain de seigle au levain, is a very well-flavoured bred, ideal with chilled oysters and fresh butter. It is very dense, tangy and with a moist interior. It should be enjoyed in thin slices with a thick layer of fresh butter and a little flaky salt. It also goes very well with air-cured meats and strong cheeses such as Roquefort. Begin by reading Baking with Levain, p. 30 (picture of the bread, p. 103).

3 loaves
Ideal dough temperature 28ºC.

1 kg fine rye flour, preferably stone ground	700 water (7 dl)
1 kg levain, see p. 31	30 g sea salt

1. Pour all the ingredients except the salt into the mixing bowl. Knead for 10 minutes on the lowest speed. Add the salt and knead at the same speed for another 5 minutes.
2. Place the dough in a lightly oiled plastic container with a lid and leave for 60 minutes.
3. Take three round baskets and dust generously with fine rye flour.
4. Turn the dough out on a floured work surface and divide into three equal pieces. Make round balls and put them seam down in the baskets. Sprinkle with rye flour and cover with a towel.
5. Leave to rise for 60–75 minutes. If you don't have any baskets, use for example three sponge cake tins. Baskets look nicer, however.
6. Preheat the oven with the stone or tray to 250º.
7. Place the three breads in the oven and spray generously with water.
8. Lower the temperature to 190ºC after 5 minutes. Open the oven door after another 10 minutes.
9. Bake for approx. 50 minutes. Use a thermometer to check that the temperature at the centre is 98ºC.
10. Take out and cool on a wire rack. Leave to settle until the next day.

Freeze in plastic bags. Defrost in the bag at room temperature.

Whole Grain Bread with Rye Kernels (p. 100).

Rye Bread with Levain (p. 101).

SAVORY BREAD

Pumpkin Bread

Wonderful with a nice bowl of soup in the autumn.

2 loaves
Ideal dough temperature 26°C.

500 g mashed pumpkin	18 g sea salt
500 g strong wheat flour, preferably stone ground	100 g pumpkin seeds
100 g wholemeal flour, preferably stone ground	100 g pumpkin seeds for the topping
150 g fine rye flour, preferably stone ground	
100 g sourdough made with wheat flour	
50 g olive oil (1.5 dl)	

1. Peel and dice a large pumpkin. Boil in water until soft and drain in a colander.
2. Purée the pumpkin flesh in a mixer. Set aside 500 g and freeze the rest.
3. Weigh the flours in a mixing bowl, dissolve the yeast in the cold pumpkin purée and pour over the flour and sourdough. Knead the dough on the lowest speed for 3 minutes and add the oil. Knead for another 7 minutes and add the salt. Increase the speed and knead vigorously for approx. 6 minutes. Test for elasticity.
4. Mix in the pumpkin seeds. Place the dough in a lightly oiled lidded plastic container. Leave for 90 minues and knock back once during rising.
5. Place on a floured work surface. Set aside 50 g for decoration and divide the rest in two.
6. Form two tight balls and cover with a tea-towel. Leave for 10 minutes.
7. Put the breads on a tea-towel dusted with flour.
8. Take a rolling pin and make eight deep indentations in the dough. Brush with a little water and dust with plenty of sifted fine rye flour. Divide the small piece of dough into two and make two balls, glaze with water and dip in pumpkin seeds. Press into the centre of the bread.
9. Cover with a tea-towel and leave to rise until doubled in size, approx. 75 minutes.
10. Preheat the oven with the stone or tray to 250°C.
11. Place the breads in the oven using a spatula and spray with plenty of water.
12. Lower the temperature to 200° after 5 minutes. Open the oven door after another 10 minutes to let some air in. Repeat twice during baking.
13. Bake for 45 minutes. Cool on wire racks.

Suitable for freezing in plastic bags.

Beetroot Bread (p. 123), Corn Bread (p. 109) and Carrot Bread in Tiger Coat (p. 164).

Corn Bread

This golden brown corn bread makes me think of New York and a deli there that served corn bread with warm sauerkraut, pastrami, mustard, pickled cucumber and lots of freshly grated horseradish. Wonderful!

2 loaves
Ideal dough temperature 26ºC.

DAY 1	DAY 2
SCALDING	KNEADING
500 g water (5 dl)	8 g yeast
375 g polenta	175 g strong wheat flour
	12 g sea salt
STARTER	1 red chilli pepper
200 g strong wheat flour	250 g tinned maize kernels
10 g yeast	
125 g water (1.25 dl)	
4 g sea salt	

DAY 1

SCALDING

Boil the water and pour over the polenta, mix with a whisk. Cover with cling-film and leave at room temperature until the following day.

STARTER

Put the flour in a mixing bowl, dissolve the yeast in the water and add to the flour. Knead for 10 minutes, add the salt and work it for another 5 minutes. Place in a lightly oiled lidded plastic container. Leave to rise in the fridge until the next day, 12–15 hours.

DAY 2

KNEADING

1. Mix the scalded flour and starter in a mixing bowl and add the yeast. Knead for half a minute (30 seconds) until the yeast has dissolved.
2. Add wheat flour and knead on low speed for 10 minutes. Add the salt and knead for another 8 minutes at slightly higher speed.
3. Remove the seeds from the chilli, dice finely and mix with the maize kernels. Stir into the dough without breaking the kernels.
4. Place the dough in a lightly oiled lidded plastic container and leave for 60 minutes. Knock back the dough after half the time.
5. Place on a floured work surface and divide in two. Form two round balls, place in a baskets sprinkled with polenta and cover with a tea-towel. Leave to rise until doubled in size at room termperature for approx. 75 minutes.
6. Preheat the oven with the stone or tray to 250ºC.
7. Place the breads in the oven using a spatula and spray generously with water.
8. Lower the temperature to 200ºC after 5 minutes. Open the oven door after another 10 minutes to let some air in. Repeat twice during baking.
9. Bake for a total of 50 minutes.
10. Remove the breads and cool on a wire rack. Spray with water for a nicely crackled surface.

Suitable for freezing in plastic bags.

Rice Baps with Salt, Chilli and Coriander (p. 120); top, Pains aux marrons (p. 124); bottom, Risotto Bread (p. 111).

Risotto Bread

The British pastry chef Richard Bingham and I created this Italian style recipe when we were guest chefs at the Vetekatten bakery in Stockholm. Cold buffet chef Linda Nilsson made a great sandwich with Italian meats and marinated vegetables. (Opposite).

To make a classic isotto you need Arborio rice, a medium, short-grain rice. It has a higher starch content than long-grained rice and absorbs more liquid during boiling without getting soggy. Other suitable types are corallo, carnaroli and vialone nano.

Use an aromatic parmesan cheese, preferably matured for four years. Always grate it yourself.

approx. 15 rolls
Ideal dough temperature 24°C.

STARTER	kneading
30 g fresh basil	15 g yeast
2 g yeast	100 g plain, low-fat
100 g water (1 dl)	yoghurt, (1 dl)
150 g strong wheat flour	256 g starter
4 g sea salt	300 g durum wheat
	100 g strong wheat flour
RISOTTO	20 g grated parmesan
200 g water (2 dl)	cheese
25 g dry white wine	8 g sea salt
(0.25 dl)	
1 vegetable stock cube	rice flour
50 g shallots	
20 g olive oil (20 ml)	
50 g Arborio rice	

STARTER

1. Rinse and finely chop the basil.
2. Dissolve the yeast in the water.
3. Add basil and wheat flour and knead for 10 minutes on low speed until elastic. Add salt and knead for 5 minutes slightly increasing the speed.
4. Test the dough for elasticity.
5. Place in a lightly oiled lidded plastic container and leave to rise at room temperature for 3 hours or over night in the fridge.

RISOTTO

6. Boil the water and white wine with the stock cube and set aside.
7. Finely chop the shallots and blanch in olive oil on low heat. Add the rice and stir for 1 minute until the rice becomes opaque.
8. Add 1/3 of the stock and simmer, stirring occasionally, until the rice starts to absorb the liquid. Add another 1/3 stock and boil for 10–12 minutes.
9. Add the remaining stock and boil. Take the saucepan off the heat and leave for 20 minutes until all liquid has been absorbed.
10. Spread the rice on a baking sheet, leave to cool.

KNEADING

1. Dissolve the yeast in the yoghurt using a whisk. Pour into a mixing bowl and add the starter, cold rice, flours and the grated cheese. Knead for 10 minutes on low speed. Add the salt and knead for another 5 minutes until the dough is elastic.
2. Place the dough in a lightly oiled lidded plastic container and leave for 60 minutes. Knock back after 30 minutes.
3. Turn out on a floured work surface. Fold into a ball without kneading. Make a sausage-shaped roll and divide into 15 pieces. Make rolls against the work top, which has been greased with 2 tbsp olive oil.
4. Sprinkle a towel with rice flower and place the buns in rows seam down. Cover a towel and leave to rise until doubled in size, approx. 45–60 minutes.
5. Preheat the oven with the stone or tray to 250°C.
6. Place the rolls in the oven floured side up and spray with generous amounts of water.
7. Lower the temperature to 200°C after 5 minutes. Open the oven door twice during baking.
8. Bake for approx. 18 minutes until golden brown.
9. Cool on a wire rack.

Suitable for freezing.

Tip
Serve with Italian food or make delicious sandwiches.

Apple Bread with Cider and Calvados

This is an fantastic bread, tangy, with a strong apple flavour and flaky crust.

2 loaves
Ideal dough temperature 24°C.

POOLISH	KNEADING
5 g yeast	6 g yeast
500 g dry French cider (3 dl)	300 g water (3 dl)
300 g strong wheat flour, preferably stone ground	600 g strong wheat flour, preferably stone ground
	100 g coarse rye flour
	18 g sea salt

Prepare the dough as for French Baguettes with Poolish, p.47.

300 g diced apple, Cox's Orange, Granny Smith or similar	10 g demerara sugar
	50 g calvados (0.5 dl)
10 g butter	4 apple slices

1. Peel, remove the pips and dice the apples. Melt butter and sugar in a frying pan and fry until golden brown. Add the calvados and boil until the mixture is dry. Leave to cool.
2. Press the mixture into the risen dough. Divide into two and form oblong loaves without first making a ball. Place on a teatowel dusted with flour and pull the cloth up between the breads.
3. Cut four thin slices of apple and press them into the centre of the loaves.
4. Cover with a towel and leave to rise until doubled in size, approx. 75 minutes.
5. Preheat the oven with the stone or tray to 250°C.
6. Place the loaves directly on the stone or tray and spray with generous amounts of water.
7. Lower the temperature to 200°C after 5 minutes. Open the oven door after another 10 minutes to let some air in.
8. Bake for 45–50 minutes. Ventilate a couple of more times during baking.
9. Take out the loaves, cool on a wire rack and spray with a little water for a crackled crust.

Suitable for freezing in plastic bags.

"Follow the instructions closely, and always use kitchen scales rather than risk inaccuracy with a decilitre or cup measure."

Walnut Bread

This wonderful walnut bread goes well with cheese or marmalade. Try to get hold of French walnuts from Grenoble, they are the best.

4 loaves
Ideal dough temperature 26°C.

STARTER
2 g yeast
100 g water (1 dl)
150 g strong wheat flour,
   preferably stone ground
2 g sea salt

KNEADING
750 g strong wheat flour,
   preferably stone ground
125 g fine rye flour,
   preferably stone ground

125 g fine rye flour,
   preferably stone ground
20 g yeast
675 g water (6.75 dl)
50 g walnut or olive oil
   (0.5 dl)
20 g sea salt
400 g walnuts

STARTER
Dissolve the yeast in the water and add the flour. Knead the dough for 10 minutes on the lowest speed. Add the salt and knead for approx. 5 minutes until the dough is elastic. Place in a lightly oiled lidded plastic container and leave to rise for 3 hours at room temperature or in the fridge over night.

KNEADING
1. Weigh the flours in a mixing bowl and add the yeast and water mixture. Add the starter.
2. Knead for 5 minutes on the lowest speed and add the oil. Knead for another 7 minutes.
3. Add the salt, increase the speed somewhat and work for another 5 minutes until elastic. Test the dough for elasticity. Coarsely crush the walnuts with a rolling pin and work into the dough.
4. Place the dough in a lightly oiled lidded plastic container and leave for 60 minutes. Knock back once.
5. Turn out on a floured work surface and divide into four pieces. Make four balls, cover with a tea-towel and leave for 10 minutes.
6. Form rectangular loaves. Place seam down in rectangular or round baskets that have been dusted with wholemeal flour or on a tea-towel generously dusted with flour. Cover with a tea-towel and leave to rise until doubled in size.
7. Preheat the oven with the stone or tray to 250°C.
8. Place thet loaves on the stone or tray and spray with generous amounts of water.
9. Lower the temperature to 200°C after 5 minutes. Open the oven door after another 10 minutes to let some air in. Repeat twice during baking.
10. Bake for a total of 50 minutes for a thick crust.
11. Take out the loaves and cool on a wire rack. Spray with water.

Do not knead too long or the gluten will lose its elastic properties.

Suitable for freezing in plastic bags.

Fruit Bread

This is the favourite bread of Christer Alfredsson at Olof Viktors, and the customers love it too. This kind of bread is very common on the continent and goes well with all kinds of cheese.

4 loaves
Ideal dough temperature 26°C.
4 rectangular cake tins

DAY 1
SOAKING
300 g dried apricots
200 g California raisins
2,000 g water (2 l)

STARTER
150 g strong wheat flour,
    preferably stone ground
2 g yeast
100 g water (1 dl)
4 g sea salt

DAY 2
KNEADING
800 g strong wheat flour,
    preferably stone ground
75 g fine wholemeal flour,
    preferably stone ground
75 g fine rye flour,
    preferably stone ground
50 g muscovado sugar
500 g water (5 dl)
20 g yeast
100 g butter
20 g sea salt

50 g wheat flour
100 g walnuts
50 g pistachios

25 g butter for greasing

DAY 1
SOAKING
Soak the dried apricots in plenty of cold water and leave for 24 hours. Soak the raisins for 30 minutes. Drain and quarter the apricots.

STARTER
Weigh the flour, dissolve the yeast in the water and pour over the flour. Knead the dough on low speed for 10 minutes. Add the salt and knead for another 5 minutes. Place the dough in a lightly oiled lidded plastic container and leave to rise for 24 hours in the fridge.

DAY 2
KNEADING
1. Mix flour and sugar in a mixing bowl. Add the starter, water and yeast and knead on low speed for 5 minutes.
2. Add butter and knead for another 5 minutes until elastic. Add the salt and knead for 5 minutes. Test the dough for elasticity.
3. Mix the drained fruit with 50 g of wheat flour, walnuts and pistachios. Mix gently to avoid breaking the fruit.
4. Place the dough in a lightly oiled lidded plastic container and leave to rise for 60 minutes, knock back once after half the time.
5. Turn out on a floured work surface, divide into four and make four round balls. Cover with a tea-towel and leave for 10 minutes.
6. Flatten the balls and form into loaves.
7. Melt the butter and use to brush 4 tins.
8. Place the loaves in the tins and sprinkle over fine rye flour.
9. Cover with a tea-towel and leave to rise for 60–75 minutes until doubled in size.
10. Preheat the oven to 250°C.
11. Place the tins in the oven and spray with generous amounts of water.
12. Lower the temperature to 180°C after 5 minutes. Open the oven door after another 10 minutes to let some air in.
13. Bake for a total of 45–50 minutes. Use a thermometer to check that the loaves are ready (98°C).
14. Take out the loaves and remove the tins.
15. Put the loaves back in the oven and bake for antoher 5 minutes.
16. Cool on a wire rack.

This wonderful bread freezes very well in plastic bags. Warm it in the oven or toast.

Almond Potato Bread

For an exotic flavour, I have added chopped chorizos and fresh rosemary to this delicious, soft and moist bread. You need nothing on it, just sprinkle with high-quality olive oil.

3 loaves
Ideal dough temperature 26°C.

250 boiled, pressed almond potatoes	500 g strong wheat flour, preferably stone ground
200 g chorizos	20 g fresh rosemary
20 g yeast	18 g sea salt
150 g water (1.5 dl)	
150 g full fat milk (1.5 dl)	

1. Boil 300 g cleaned almond potatoes until soft. Pour away the water and let the remaining water evaporate on the stove. Peel the potatoes with a small knife and press. Cool.
2. Dice the chorizos and set aside.
3. Dissolve the yeast in the water and milk and pour over the flour.
4. Rub off the fresh rosemary into the bowl and add the pressed potatoes. Knead for 10 minutes on low speed. Add salt and increase the speed. Knead for another 5 minutes until elastic. Test the dough for elasticity.
5. Mix in the diced sausage. Place the dough in a lightly oiled lidded plastic container and leave for 120 minutes, knock back twice during rising.
6. Turn out on a floured work top make a coil and cut into 15 pieces. Make rolls.
7. Sift a little flour into three round baskets and place the rolls inside. You can also put them straight on the tray and sift over some wheat flour.
8. Cover with a tea-towel and leave to rise for 60–75 minutes until doubled in size.
9. Preheat the oven with the stone or tray to 250°C.
10. Remove the baskets and put two of the loaves in the oven. Put the third in the fridge to avoid it rising too much. Spray with generous amounts of water.
11. Lower the temperature to 200°C after 5 minutes. Open the oven door after another 10 minutes to let some air in. Repeat twice during baking.
12. Take out the loaves and place on a wire rack. Spray with water for a nice crackled crust.
13. Cool on a wire rack.

Suitable for freezing in plastic bags.

"You can use almost anything that tastes nice to add flavour to bread."

Almond Potato Bread, Vegetable Bread and Rolls (p. 131)

Rice Baps with Salted Lemon, Chilli and Coriander

This light, fluffy bread goes very well with Asian food, or use as a sandwich base. The salted lemon gives it a wonderful, fresh flavour. (Picture on p. 110)

approx. 15 baps
Ideal dough temperature 26°C.

SALTED LEMON	DAY 2
5 lemons, yellow and ripe	20 g finely chopped
100 g sugar	coriander
200 g sea salt	100 g salted lemon
200 g water (2 dl)	10 g red chillies

DAY 1	KNEADING
SCALDING THE RICE	230 g cold scalded rice
65 g rice flour	15 g yeast
200 g water (2 dl)	150 g water (1.5 dl)
	100 g durum wheat
The scalded rice will weigh	30 g fine rye flour,
230 g.	preferably stone ground
	15 g butter
	15 g sea salt

THREE DAYS AHEAD OF BAKING

SALTED LEMON

1. Wash the lemons carefully using a brush and tepid water. Quarter and peel the lemons. Squeeze out the juice and use it for making sorbet or lemonade.
2. Boil 2 l of water in a 4 l saucepan. Add the rinds and boil with a lid for 5 minutes. Rinse. Repeat three times, changing the water each time to remove all bitterness.
3. Place the rinds in a large glass jar. For the syrup, whisk together sugar, salt and boiling water. Pour over the rinds and leave at room temperature for at least three days until the rinds are soft and delicious. The same method can be used for lime and grapefruit rinds.

DAY 1

SCALDING

Put the rice flour in a 1 l bowl. Boil the water and pour over the flour. Whisk into a smooth batter. Cover with cling-film, cool and put in the fridge until the next day.

DAY 2

Rinse, dry and finely chop the coriander. Rinse the lemon rinds under the tap, pat them dry with kitchen paper and chop finely. Rinse and cut the chilli lengthways. Remove the seeds and dice finely.

KNEADING

1. Place the scalded rice in a mixing bowl. Dissolve the yeast in the water and pour over the rice. Add the other ingredients except salt. Knead for 10 minutes on the lowest speed. Add the salt and knead for another 5–10 minutes at slightly higher speed. Place the dough in a lightly oiled lidded plastic container and leave for 90 minutes.
2. Turn out on a floured work top and roll out to a rope, cut 80 g pieces and make rolls. Place these on a tea-towel dusted with flour and cover with another tea-towel. Leave for 15 minutes.
3. Make round flat cakes the size of a saucer from the rice flour. Place on a tea-towel dusted with flour and sift over rice flour. Cover and leave to rise for approx. 45 minutes until doubled in size.
4. Preheat the oven with the stone or tray to 250°C.
5. Place the breads in the oven and spray with water.
6. Bake for approx. 12 minutes until golden brown.
7. Remove from the oven and cool on a wire rack.

Chilli and Cheddar Bread (p. 143).

Nettle Triangles

Nettles, aniseed and finely chopped chives are ideal flavour enhancers. If you cannot get hold of nettles use parsley.

2 loaves
Ideal dough temperature 24°C.

POOLISH
Rising time 1 h at room temperature or 15–20 hours in the fridge.
5 g yeast
200 g water, 20°C (2 dl)
150 g rye sourdough, p.29
190 g dinkel flour
110 g fine rye flour, preferably stone ground

100 g nettles
100 g chives

KNEADING
10 g yeast
300 g water, 20°C (3 dl)
400 g strong wheat flour, preferably stone ground
240 g wholemeal flour, preferably stone ground
20 g honey
5 g aniseed
20 g sea salt

POOLISH
Dissolve the yeast in the water, add the sourdough and flour. Cover with cling-film and leave to rise at room temperature for 3 hours or overnight in the fridge.

Parboil the nettles or parsley in boiling water. Rinse in cold water and squeeze out the liquid. Finely chop and put in a mixer together with the chives.

KNEADING
1. Dissolve the yeast in the water using a whisk, add poolish, flour, honey, nettles, chives and aniseed.
2. Knead the dough on the lowest speed for 13 minutes. Add the salt, increase the speed and knead for another 8 minutes until elastic.
3. Place the dough in a lightly oiled lidded plastic container and leave to rise for 75 minutes. Knock back once during rising.
4. Turn out on a floured work surface, divide in two and form two balls. Place on a tea-towel dusted with flour, cover and leave for 10 minutes.
5. Place one of the balls on the work surface and roll out three "tongues", approx. 5 cm long. Fold up over the ball. Place on a tea-towel dusted with fine rye flour, "tongues" down. Cover and leave to rise for 45–60 minutes until doubled in size.
6. Preheat the oven with the stone or tray to 250°C.
7. Put the loaves in the oven right side up. Spray generously with water.
8. Lower the temperature to 200°C after 5 minutes. Open the oven door after another 10 minutes to let some air in. Repeat twice during baking.
9. Take out the bread after 40 minutes and cool on a wire rack.

Because of their shape, these breads dry out easily and are not suitable for freezing. If you want to freeze them, make loaves instead.

Beetroot Bread

Add dill to these attractive and tasty breads and eat with crayfish, or add diced chèvre towards the end of mixing the dough. (See picture p. 108 and this page).

2 or 4 loaves depending on shape
Ideal dough temperature 24°C.

WHITE DOUGH
5 g yeast
100 g water (1 dl)
170 g strong wheat flour,
    preferably stone ground
4 g sea salt

BEETROOT DOUGH
150 g grated raw beetroot
350 g water (3.5 dl)
15 g yeast
25 g honey
100 g fine rye flour,
    preferably stone ground
750 g strong wheat flour,
    preferably stone ground
20 g salt

Top with flaky salt and
caraway seeds.

WHITE DOUGH
Dissolve the yeast in the water, pour the mixture over the flour and knead on the lowest speed for 13 minutes. Add the salt, increase the speed somewhat and knead for another 7 minutes. Place the dough in a lightly oiled lidded plastic container and leave for 60–90 minutes. Knock back once during rising.

BEETROOT DOUGH
1. Wash and grate the fresh beetroot, mix with water, yeast and honey in a bowl. Add the flour and knead on the lowest speed for 13 minutes. Add the salt, increase the speed and work for another
7 minutes. Test the dough for elasticity.
2. Place the dough in a lightly oiled lidded plastic container and leave for 60–90 minutes. Knock down after half the time.
3. There are two different shapes, as shown in the picture.
• To make the large bread, divide the beetroot dough in half and make two round balls. Then divide the white dough in half, roll out a flat ribbon and place it round the bread, seam down. Finally, spray or brush with water and sift wheat flour over the top.

• To make the bread at the top of the picture, divide the beetroot dough into four and make round, taut balls. Then divide the white dough into four and roll out flat cakes. Brush these with water and place on top of the bread. Glaze again and sprinkle with caraway seeds and flaky salt.
4. Place on a tea-towel dusted with flour, cover and leave to rise for 60–75 minutes or until doubled in size.
5. Preheat the oven with the stone or tray to 250°C.
6. Place the breads in the oven and spray generously with water.
7. Lower the temperature to 200°C after 5 minutes. Open the oven door after another 10 minutes to let some air in. Repeat twice during baking.
8. Bake the two large, round loaves for 50 minutes and the smaller for 40 minutes.
9. Take out the loaves and place on a wire rack. Spray with water for a crackled surface.

Chestnut Bread

Chestnut flour, or *farine de châtaigne* as it is called in France, has many uses. This bread goes very well with game or fine air-cured ham.

The chestnut flour can be replaced with buckwheat flour. The result is not quite the same, but still delicious.

approx. 35 rolls
Ideal dough temperature 26°C.

STARTER	KNEADING
375 strong wheat flour, preferably stone ground	250 g chestnut flour
3 g yeast	600 g strong wheat flour, preferably stone ground
225 g water (1.25 dl)	25 g set honey
	25 g yeast
	275 g water (2.75 dl)
	25 g sea salt
	150 g pine nuts or 250 g peeled, chopped, fresh chestnuts

Preheat the oven to 200°C and roast the pine nuts until golden brown, giving them an occasional stir. If you use chestnuts, cut a cross across the top and bake for 30 minutes. Remove the shell and skin and chop coarsely.

STARTER
Weigh the flour in a mixing bowl. Dissolve the yeast in the water and pour over the flour. Knead the dough on low speed for 10 minutes. Place the dough in a lightly oiled lidded plastic container and leave to rise for 3 hours at room temperature or in the fridge overnight.

KNEADING
1. Weigh the flours, add starter and honey. Dissolve the yeast in the water with a whisk and pour over the flour. Knead on low speed for 10 minutes. Add the salt, increase the speed and work for approx. 8 minutes until elastic. Test the dough for elasticity.
2. Place the dough in a lightly oiled lidded plastic container and leave for 45 minutes, knock back once during rising.

3. If you are making loaves, divide the dough in two, make two round balls and leave them to rise until doubled in size on a tea-towel dusted with flour, approx. 60 minutes. Brush with water, sift generously with chestnut flour and cut the top with a pair of scissors so they look like chestnuts.
4. Place on greased trays and leave to rise for 60 minutes until doubled in size.
5. Preheat the oven to 250°C. Place the breads in the oven and spray generously with water.
6. Lower the temperature to 200°C after 5 minutes. Open the oven door after another 10 minutes to let some air in. Repeat twice during baking.
7. Bake for a total of 50 minutes.
8. The rolls are made in the same way as the loaves, but the oven temperature should be 250°C and the baking time 8–12 minutes.
9. Cool on a wire rack.

Suitable for freezing. Defrost and heat before serving and they are as good as new.

The texture is slightly different, a bit like rye bread, since the chestnut flour contains no gluten and only 0.5% fat.

Pain aux marrons

I once tasted a wonderful chestnut bread in a small bakery down in a harbour on Corsica. I invited the baker and his wife to visit the bakery on board the boat where I was working. The baker gave us permission to use his recipe on condition that I brought him a sugar sculpture for his window display the next time I came to Corsica

This bread is baked with levain, which means that you need to have a batch in the fridge, see p. 31. You need to prepare this dough in good time before baking. It may seem more trouble than it is worth, but the result will convince you otherwise. (See picture on p. 110).

Continued on p. 126.

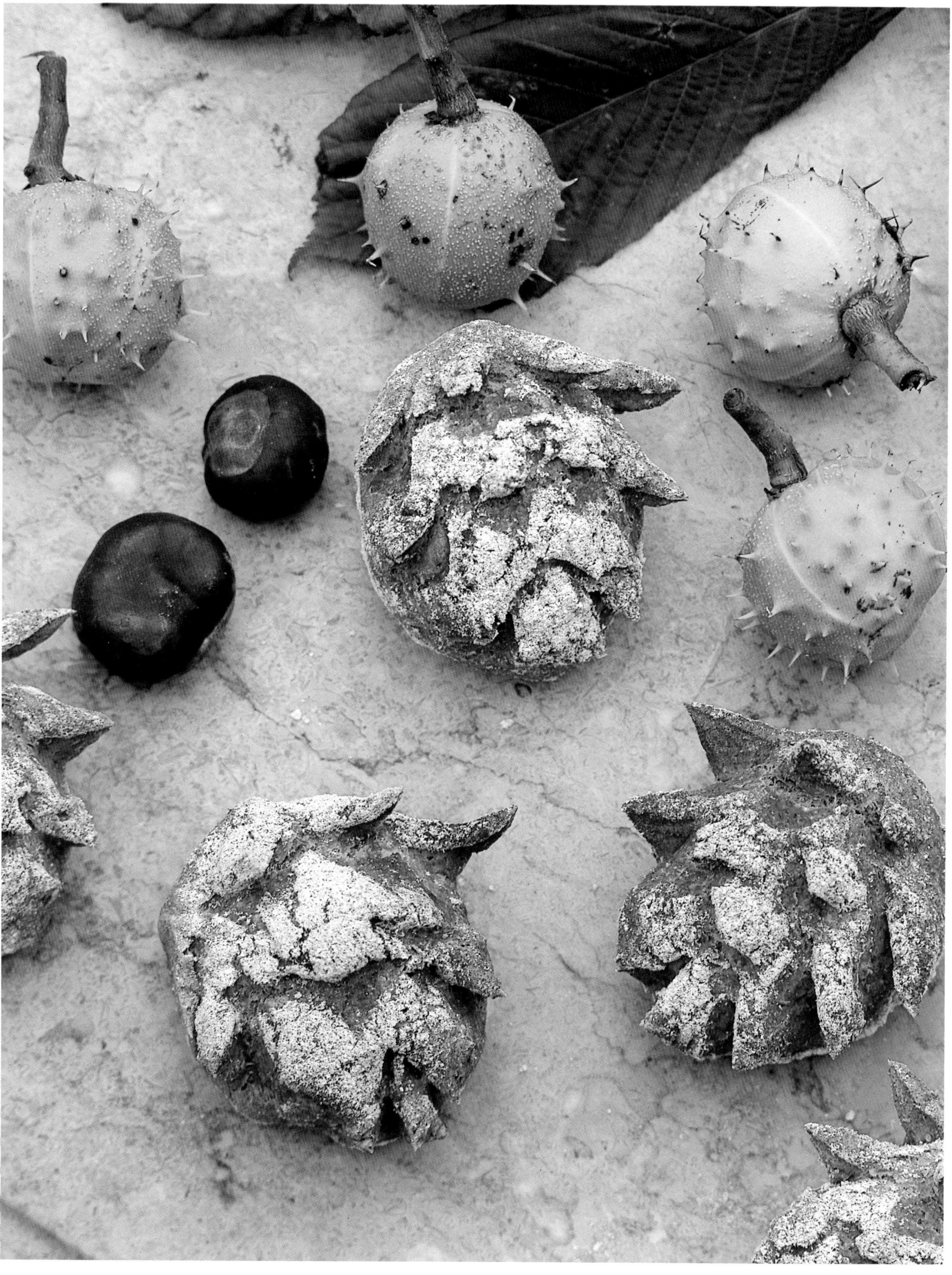

Chestnut Bread.

If you want to use only levain, omit the yeast and leave to rise for 170 minutes.

2 loaves
Ideal dough temperature 28°C.

500 g chestnuts

CHESTNUT PURÉE

1. Put 500 g chestnuts on a square low-edged tin, cut a cross across the top and roast until they open, approx. 30 minutes.
2. Cool and peel with a small knife. Remove both the shell and the skin.
3. Purée 100 g of the chestnuts. Crush the rest using a rolling pin.

12 g yeast	100 chestnut purée
400 g water (4 dl)	20 g sea salt
460 g levain, see p. 31	
260 g fine rye flour	280 g peeled, crushed
300 g strong wheat flour	chestnuts

1. Dissolve the yeast in the water, add levain, flours and chestnut purée. Knead for 13 minutes on low speed. Add salt and work for 5 minutes. Test the dough for elasticity. Gently mix in the chestnuts. Avoid kneading the dough for too long.
2. Place in a lightly oiled lidded plastic container and leave for 90 minutes, knock back once.
3. Turn out on a floured work surface.
4. Divide the dough in two and shape balls. Roll out a rectangle and fold in three. Place seam down in two round baskets dusted with coarse-ground rye flour. Sift rye flour over the top and cover with a tea-towel.
5. Leave to rise until doubled in size. 90 minutes depending on the room temperature.
6. Preheat the oven with the stone or tray to 250°C.
7. Place the loaves in the oven and spray generously with water.
8. Lower the temperature to 200°C after 5 minutes. Open the oven door after another 10 minutes to let some air in. Repeat twice during baking.
9. Bake for a total of 60 minutes.
10. Take out the bread and cool on a wire rack.

Suitable for freezing in plastic bags.

Lemon Bread

I call these breads Délices au citron when I work as a guest chef. The first time I made it was on the cruise liner M/S Vistafjord where we served it with seafood and fish soup.

Do not add lemon juice to the dough or it will get too loose.

Ideal dough temperature 26°C.

DAY 1	650 g strong wheat flour,
STARTER	preferably stone ground
100 g fine rye flour,	15 g yeast
preferably stone ground	250 g water (2.5 dl)
150 g durum wheat	50 g green virgin olive oil
10 g yeast	of the best quality
250 g water (2.5 dl)	(0.5 dl)
	20 g sea salt
DAY 2	
KNEADING	Polenta flour for the
2 yellow, ripe lemons,	topping
preferably organic	

DAY 1

STARTER

Dissolve the yeast in the water and pour the mixture over the flours. Knead the dough for 10 minutes on low speed. Place the dough in a lightly oiled lidded plastic container and leave in the fridge over night.

DAY 2

KNEADING

1. Wash and dry the lemons. Grate the yellow part only.
2. Weigh the flour in a bowl and add the starter and lemon rind.
3. Dissolve the yeast in the water and pour over the flour
4. Knead on low speed for 3 minutes. Add the oil and knead for another 10 minutes, then add the salt.
5. Increase the speed somewhat and knead for 7 minutes until elastic. Test the dough for elasticity.
6. Place the dough in a lightly oiled lidded plastic container and leave for 90 minutes, knock back once.

Continued on p. 128

Lemon Bread.

7. Divide into four. Make round balls, cover by a tea-towel and leave for 10 minutes.
8. Make short loaves with tapering ends, like lemons
9. Brush with water and dip the breads in polenta flour.
10. Leave to rise on a tea-towel dusted with flour. Pull up the cloth between the breads so that they rise upwards, not sideways. Cover with another tea-towel and leave to rise for 60 minutes until doubled in size.

Rolls

7. Roll out the dough, cut off 25 g pieces and make rolls. Cover with a tea-towel and leave for 5 minutes.
8. Make oblong, lemon-shaped rolls tapering at the ends.
9. Brush or spray with water.
10. Place on a baking tray, cover with a tea-towel and leave to rise for 60 minutes until doubled in size.
11. Preheat the oven with the stone or tray to 250°C.
12. Place the rolls in the oven and spray generously with water.
13. Lower the temperature to 200°C after 5 minutes. Open the oven door after another 10 minutes to let some air in. Repeat twice during baking.
14. Bake for a total of 45 minutes for the loaves. Bake the rolls at the same temperature for 12 minutes until golden brown.
15. Take out the bread and place them on a wire rack, spray with water.
16. Cool on a wire rack.

Tip
Suitable for freezing. Defrost and heat up as an accompaniment to, for example, shellfish.

Glasswort and Nori Seaweed Bread

This bread goes well with my favourite foods – fish and shellfish. Glasswort comes in different colours. It can be bought from well-stocked delicatessens, farmers markets or order it at the greengrocer's. It is wonderfully salty and tastes of the sea.

4 loaves

Make the dough as for Lemon Bread, p. 126
200 g glasswort
1 packet nori sheets

1. Dice the glasswort.
2. Mix in the glasswort after you have finished kneading the lemon bread dough.
3. Place the dough in a lightly oiled lidded plastic container and leave for 90 minutes, knock back once during rising.
4. Turn out on a floured work surface and cut into four pieces. Make dough balls with the help of a little wheat flour, cover with a towel and leave for 10 minutes.
5. Roll back and forth at the centre of the dough ball to form a "lip" with a thin centre and thicker sides.
6. Place the dough on two greased trays, fold over the "lip" and press the rolling pin into the centre. Make eight cuts on the side of the bread. Fold over after placing it on the tray.
7. Take out a nori sheet and divide into two. Dip one half in a bowl of water and wrap it around the bread with the seam underneath. Repeat with the other breads.
8. Dust with wheat flour, cover with a teatowel and leave to rise until doubled in size, approx. 75 minutes depending on the room temperature.
9. Preheat the oven to 250°C.
10. Put one tray in a cool place and the other in the oven. Spray generously with water.
11. Lower the temperature to 200°C after 5 minutes. Open the oven door after another 10 minutes to let some air in. Repeat twice during baking.
12. Take out the breads and cool on a wire rack.

Tip
Bread for a buffet can be made well ahead and frozen in plastic bags. Defrost in the bag, heat for 5 minutes at 200°C.

Glasswort and Nori Seaweed Bread.

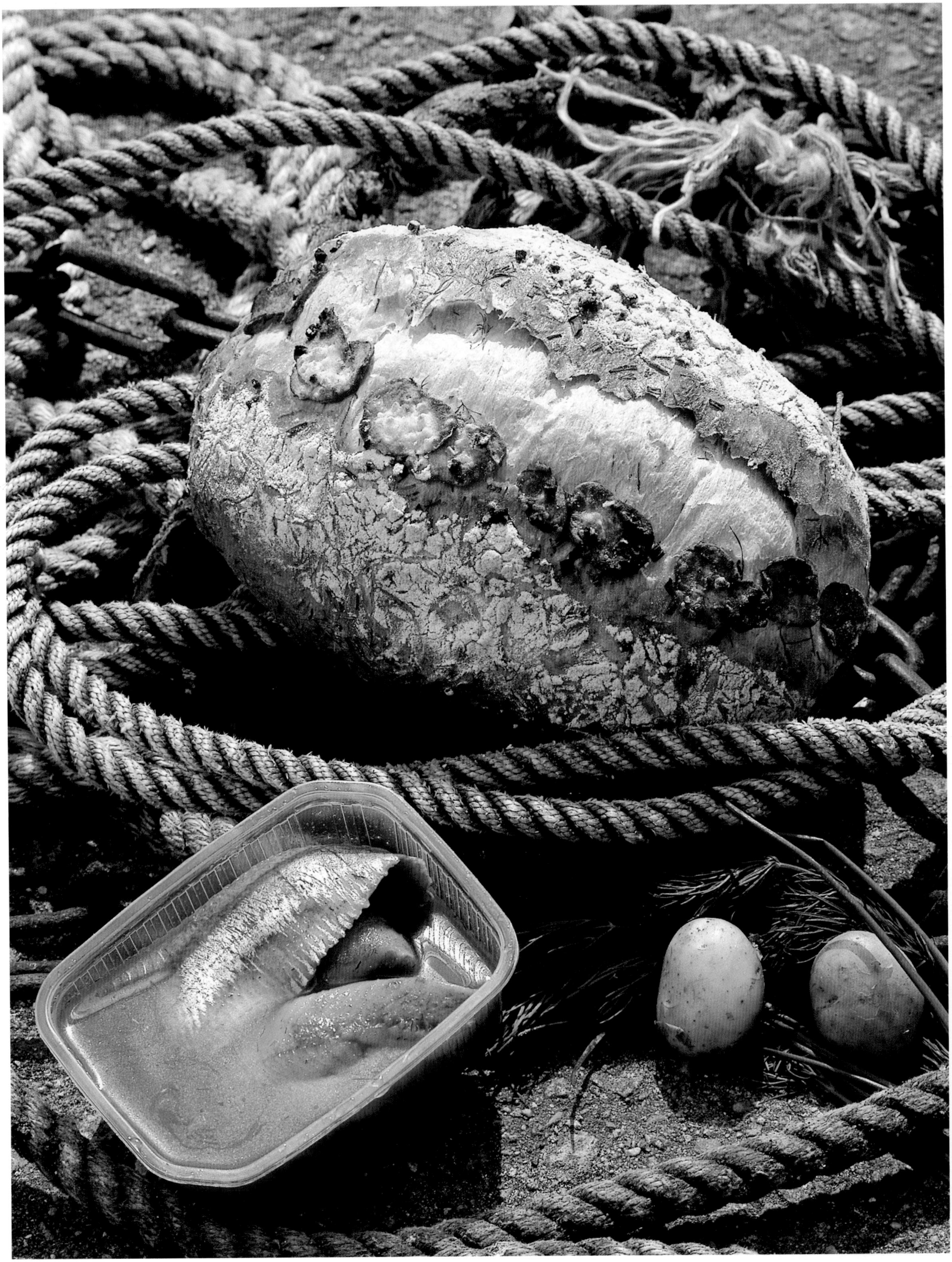

Summer Bread.

Summer Bread

Summer bread (left). Great with pickled herring and schnapps.

2 large or 4 small loaves
Ideal dough temperature 26°C.

500 g scrubbed, peeled and boiled new potatoes
900 g strong wheat flour, preferably stone ground
25 g yeast
500 g water (5 dl)

50 g rapeseed oil (0.5 dl)
20 g sea salt
25 g dill, chopped
25 g chives, finely chopped
flaky salt for the topping

1. Dice the boiled, cold potatoes. Save two for the topping.
2. Measure the flour, dissolve the yeast in the water and mix. Knead the dough on the lowest speed for 3 minutes. Add oil and knead for 12 minutes. Add the salt, increase the speed and knead for 5 minutes until elastic. Test the dough for elasticity.
3. Gently mix in the potatoes, dill and chives. Place the dough in a lightly oiled lidded plastic container and leave for 2 hours.
4. Turn out on a floured work surface and make two tight balls of dough, cover with a tea-towel and leave for 10 minutes.
5. Flatten the breads with your hand and fold into two long loaves. Place seam down in two rectangular baskets generously dusted with wheat flour. Sift a little wheat flour over the breads to prevent the towel from sticking. Leave to rise for approx. 75 minutes until doubled in size.
6. Preheat the oven with the stone or tray to 250°C.
7. Turn out on a tea-towel dusted with flour and brush the centre with water. Slice the potatoes thin, place on top of the breads and sprinkle with flaky salt.
8. Place the breads in the oven and spray generously with water.
9. Lower the temperature to 200°C after 5 minutes. Open the oven door after another 10 minutes to let some air in. Repeat twice during baking.
10. Bake for 40 minutes.
11. Cool on a wire rack.

This is enough for two large loaves. If you want them smaller, divide the dough into four pieces instead of two. They freeze well, but without the potato topping.

Vegetable Bread

Make this pretty and delicious summer bread when fresh vegetables are in season. (Picture on p. 119)

2 loaves or approx. 20 rolls
Ideal dough temperature 27°C.

500 g mixed vegetables, e.g. carrots, cauliflower, string beans, peas or mange-touts
25 g parsley
25 g chives
20 g yeast
250 g milk (2.5 dl)
50 g fine rye flour

400 g strong wheat flour, preferably stone ground
50 g durum wheat
25 g olive oil (0.25 dl)
10 g salt

durum wheat for the topping

1. Bring lightly salted water to the boil and parboil each vegetable separately. Cool in ice water. The mange-touts only need a few seconds, the peas can be frozen and simply defrosted. Defrosted frozen summer greens works too. Pat dry with kitchen paper.
2. Rinse and chop the parsley. Cut the chives in small pieces, do not chop it.
3. Dissolve the yeast in the milk and pour over the flour, parsley and chives. Knead the dough on low speed for 3 minutes. Add the oil and knead for another 11 minutes. Add the salt, increase the speed and knead for another 6 minutes until elastic. Test the dough for elasticity.
4. Place in a lightly oiled lidded plastic container and leave for 60 minutes, knock back after 30 min.
5. Turn out on a floured work surface.

6. *To make rolls*: Roll out the dough into a sausage shape using durum wheat and cut off 80 g pieces. Place in a greased tin or on a tea-towel and rise for 45–60 minutes until doubled in size.
7. Preheat the oven to 250°C. Put the tray in the oven and spray the rolls generously with water.
8. Bake for approx. 15 minutes until brown.
9. Cool on a wire rack.

6. *To make bread*: Divide the dough into six pieces and make round dough balls. Place in two floured rectangular baskets, sprinkle with flour and cover.

Continued on p. 133.

Asparagus Bread with Parmesan Cheese and Walnuts.

Alternatively, place the pieces side by side on the tray and sprinkle with wheat flour. Cover and leave to rise for approx. 60 minutes until doubled in size.

7. Preheat the oven with the stone or tray to 250°C. Place the breads in the oven and spray generously with water.

8. Lower the temperature to 200°C after 5 minutes. Open the oven door after another 10 minutes to let some air in. Repeat twice during baking.

9. Bake for 40 minutes.

10. Remove the breads and cool on a wire rack.

Not suitable for freezing.

Asparagus Bread with Parmesan Cheese and Walnuts

This lovely bread goes well with a cold meat and salad buffet.

4 loaves
Ideal dough temperature 26°C.

250 g green asparagus	25 g yeast
50 g rocket	500 g water (5 dl)
100 g walnuts, preferably French	50 g olive oil (0.5 dl)
	20 g sea salt
100 g freshly grated parmesan cheese	
900 g strong wheat flour, preferably stone ground	

1. Bring 1 l of water to the boil with a pinch of sea salt. Cut each asparagus stick into six pieces. Boil for 2 minutes, place in a colander and rinse under cold running water.

2. Boil the rocket for a couple of seconds. Rinse under cold running water.

3. Chop the rocket coarsely and cut the asparagus into small pieces. Crush the walnuts coarsely with a rolling pin and grate the mature parmesan.

4. Measure the flour, dissolve the yeast in the water and pour over the flour. Knead on the lowest speed for 3 minutes. Add the olive oil and knead for 12 minutes. Add the salt, increase the speed somewhat and work for

5 minutes until very elastic. Add asparagus, rocket, walnuts and parmesan and mix carefully.

5. Place the dough in a lightly oiled lidded plastic container and leave for 2 hours.

6. Turn out on a floured work surface and divide into four.

7. Make round balls. Cover with a tea-towel and leave for 10 minutes.

8. Flatten the balls with your hand and fold into taut breads with slightly tapering ends. Place on a floured baking towel. Sprinkle with wheat flour and cover with a tea-towel. Pull up the cloth between the breads to support the dough. Leave to rise for approx. 75 minutes until doubled in size.

9. Preheat the oven with the stone or tray to 250°C.

10. Place the breads directly on the stone or tray and spray generously with water. This dough rises slowly, so the bread can wait in room temperature while the others are in the oven.

11. Lower the temperature to 200°C after 5 minutes. Open the oven door after another 10 minutes to let some air in. Repeat twice during baking.

12. Bake for 40–45 minutes and cool on a wire rack.

13. Bake the remaining breads.

Basil Bread.

Basil Bread

This delicious bread made with yoghurt and chopped basil or lots of dill is delicious accompaniment to a shellfish buffet. I sometimes use mushrooms fried in butter and a little finely chopped chives. A little grated orange or lemon zest makes the dough even more interesting. (Opposite).

2 loaves
Ideal dough temperature 26°C.

DAY 1	250 g plain yoghurt
POOLISH	(2.5 dl)
3 g yeast	450 g strong wheat flour,
250 g water (2.5 dl)	preferably stone ground
250 g durum wheat	40 g egg yolk (2 eggs)
	20 g rinsed and finely
DAY 2	chopped basil
KNEADING	18 g sea salt
30 g yeast	
50 g set honey	

DAY 1

POOLISH

Dissolve the yeast in the water, add the durum flour and whisk to a smooth batter. Cover with cling-film and leave at room temperature for 24 hours.

DAY 2

KNEADING

1. Dissolve the yeast in the honey and yoghurt and pour over the flour. Add egg yolk, basil and poolish.
2. Work the dough on the lowest speed for 13 minutes. Add the salt and increase the speed. Knead the dough for 7 minutes until elastic.
3. Place in a lightly oiled lidded plastic container. Leave for 60 minutes. Knock back after 30 minutes.
4. Turn out on a floured work surface and divide into two.
5. Make round balls and cover. Leave for 10 minutes. Knock back the dough and make two loaves.
6. Leave them to rise on a tea-towel dusted with flour, sift over some wheat flour and cover. Leave to rise for 60–75 minutes until doubled in size.
7. Preheat the oven with the stone or tray to 250°C.
8. Pick up the breads on a spatula and slash a couple of times with a sharp knife or razor blade.
9. Place the breads in the oven and spray generously with water.
10. Lower the temperature to 200°C after 5 minutes. Open the oven door after another 10 minutes to let some air in. Repeat twice during baking.
11. Bake for a total of 50 minutes.
12. Take out the breads, place on a wire rack and spray with water for an attractive crackled surface.

Arame Seaweed Bread

This bread goes well with shellfish and a glass of dry Chablis. Seaweed can be bought in health food shops, delicatessens or Asian markets. (Picture on p. 136).

2 loaves

1 batch basil bread dough
2 limes
25 g arame + seaweed for topping

Use the same dough as for Basil Bread, omitting the basil and add the grated zest of two washed and dried limes.

1. Add 25 g arame towards the end of kneading.
2. Place the dough in a lightly oiled lidded plastic container and leave for 60 minutes, knock back once during rising.
3. Turn out on a floured work surface and divide into two.
4. Flatten the pieces, put arame on top and fold in three. Sprinkle wheat flour on a tea-towel and place the breads on it seam down. Cover with a tea-towel and leave to rise for 60–70 minutes until doubled in size.
5. Preheat the oven with the stone or tray to 250°C.
6. Turn over the breads seam up, place in the oven and spray generously with water.
7. Lower the temperature to 200°C after 5 minutes. Open the oven door after another 10 minutes to let some air in. Repeat twice during baking.
8. Bake for 55–60 minutes.
9. Take out the breads and cool on a wire rack.

Suitable for freezing in plastic bags.

Arame Seaweed Bread (p. 135).

Jerusalem Artichoke Bread (p. 138).

Jerusalem Artichoke Bread

The artichokes add a very distinctive flavour. Use the same dough as for Pain de campagne traditionnel (see p. 83). There are many ways of flavouring this basic dough. It contains levain, so begin by reading the instructions on p. 30, Baking with Levain. (Picture p. 137).

3 loaves

300 g Jerusalem artichokes
50 g butter
salt and pepper

1 batch Pain de campagne traditionnel dough, see p. 83

1. Clean, peel and dice the Jerusalem artichokes finely.
2. Heat in butter until they start to turn brown. Add salt and pepper. Cool completely before adding to the dough.
3. Prepare the dough according to the instructions on p. 83, then add the Jerusalem artichokes.
4. Place the dough in a lightly oiled lidded plastic container and leave for 120 minutes.
5. Turn out on a flourred work surface and divide into three.
6. Make round balls. Sprinkle plenty of wheat flour on a tea-towel and place the breads on it seam down. Cover with another towel and leave to rise for aprox. 120 minutes depending on the room temperature, or until doubled in size.
7. Preheat the oven with the stone or tray to 250°C.
8. Turn over two of the loaves seam up and place in the oven. Spray generously with water. Put the third bread in the fridge and bake it after the two first.
9. Lower the temperature to 200°C after 5 minutes. Open the oven door after another 10 minutes to let some air in. Repeat twice during baking.
10. Bake for a total of 60 minutes.
11. Take out the loaves, place on a wire rack and spray with water for a nice crackled surface.

Suitable for freezing in plastic bags.

Rhubarb Bread

This bread is based on the classic Pain de campagne (see p. 83). I started making this at Easter, 2002. Both we at Olof Viktors and our customers loved it. The dough contains levain, so begin by reading the instructions on p. 30, Baking with Levain.

3 loaves

600 g rhubarb, weighed
   after washing and peeling
150 g sugar

1 batch Pain de campagne traditionnel dough, p. 83.

DAY 1
Peel the rhubarb, make long strips from 300 g, put in a plastic bag in the fridge until the next day. Dice the rest. Mix with the sugar, put under pressure and leave at room temperature until the next day.

DAY 2
1. Drain the rhubarb and pat it dry with kitchen paper.
2. Prepare the dough, then fold in the rhubarb.
3. Place the dough in a lightly oiled lidded plastic container and leave for 120 minutes.
4. Turn out on a floured work surface and divide into three. Make three taut buns, cover with a tea-towel and leave for 10 minutes.
5. Flatten the buns with your hand and shape three oblong, short breads. Put two of them on a greased baking tray and the third on another.
6. Take out the rhubarb strips and cut them into suitable lengths. Wrap these round the breads, seam down, see the picture on the opposite page. Sprinkle with fine rye flour and cover.
7. Leave to rise for approx. 120 minutes until doubled in size.
8. Preheat the oven to 250°C.
9. Put the first tray in the oven and spray generously with water while the other rest in the fridge.
10. Lower the temperature to 200°C after 5 minutes. Open the oven door after another 10 minutes to let some air in. Repeat twice during baking.
11. Bake for a total of 50 minutes.
12. Take out the breads and cool on a wire rack. Repeat with the other tray.

Suitable for freezing in plastic bags.

Cheese Bread (p. 160).

Garlic Bread (p. 142), Rolls (p. 21) and Spinach Bread (pp. 150, 153).

Garlic Bread

These wonderfully crusty breads go well with food and are ideal for making delicious sandwiches. Remember to add the garlic towards the end. Garlic is rich in ascorbic acid, vitamin C, which means that the dough will get too loose if added at the start. (Picture p. 141 top left).

4 loaves
Ideal dough temperature 26ºC.

15 g yeast	100 g sourdough made with
600 g water (6 dl)	wheat flour, see p. 29
700 g strong wheat flour,	10 g herbes de Provence
preferably stone ground	18 g sea salt
150 g fine rye flour,	30 g crushed garlic
preferably stone ground	50 g olive oil (0.5 dl)

1. Dissolve the yeast in the water and pour the mixture over the flour, sourdough and herbs.
2. Knead on the lowest speed for 13 minutes. Add the salt, increase the speed and knead for 7 minutes until it no longer sticks to the side of the bowl.
3. Crush the garlic with a pestle and mortar and add the oil. Mix in the garlic.
4. Place the dough in a lightly oiled lidded plastic container and leave for 90–120 minutes. Knock back twice during rising.
5. Turn out on a floured work surface and divide into four equal pieces. Make buns, cover with a tea-towel and leave for 10 minutes.
6. Make an indentation in the centre using a rolling pin. Fold into three and place the buns seam down on a tea-towel dusted with flour. Sprinkle with wheat flour, cover and leave to rise for 90 minutes until doubled in size.
7. Preheat the oven with the stone or tray to 250ºC.
8. Slash the buns (see p. 141) with a sharp knife.
9. Place in the oven and spray generously with water.
10. Lower the temperature to 200ºC after 5 minutes. Open the oven door after another 10 minutes to let some air in. Repeat twice during baking.
11. Bake for a total of 50 minutes.
12. Take out the bread, place on a wire rack and spray with water. Cool on a wire rack.

Suitable for freezing in plastic bags.

Blueberry Bread

I call this Winnie-the-Pooh bread since it contains things that Winnie-the-Pooh likes. (Picture p. 144).

3 loaves
Ideal dough temperature 26ºC.
3 rectangular baking tins

DAY 1	DAY 2
STARTER	KNEADING
3 g yeast	20 g yeast
150 g water (1.5 dl)	400 g water (4 dl)
250 g strong wheat flour,	620 g strong wheat flour,
preferably stone ground	preferably stone ground
4 g sea salt	100 g fine rye flour,
	preferably stone ground
	60 g set honey
	200 g blueberries
	40 g butter
	16 g sea salt
	120 g walnuts, crushed
	25 g butter for greasing

DAY 1

STARTER

Dissolve the yeast in the water and pour the mixture over the flour. Knead on low speed for 13 minutes. Add the salt and work for another 2 minutes. Place the dough in a lightly oiled lidded plastic container and leave in the fridge over night.

DAY 2

KNEADING

1. Dissolve the yeast in the water, add the starter, flour, honey and blueberries.
2. Knead on low speed for 3 minutes, add the butter and work for another 11 minutes. Add the salt and knead until the dough no longer sticks to the side of the bowl, approx. 6 minutes. Test the dough for elasticity. Mix in the coarsely crushed walnuts.
3. Place in a lightly oiled lidded plastic container and leave for 60 minutes. Knock back after 30 min.
4. Turn out on a floured work surface, divide into three.
5. Form rectangular loaves and place in the greased tins that should be half full.

6. Sprinkle with wheat flour and leave to rise for approx. 60 minutes until doubled in size. Cut a diamond pattern across the top with a sharp knife.
7. Preheat the oven to 250°C.
8. Put the tins in the oven and spray with water.
9. Lower the temperature to 180°C after 5 minutes. Open the oven door after another 10 minutes to let some air in. Repeat twice during baking.
10. Bake for approx. 40 minutes. Check the temperature at the centre, it should be 98°C.
11. Turn out on the work surface, place on a tray and bake for another 5 minutes for a harder crust.
12. Cool on a wire rack.

Suitable for freezing in plastic bags. Defrost in the bag and heat in the oven before serving.

Chilli and Cheddar Bread

In this recipe, the flavour of the cheddar blends with the other aromatic ingredients. This crusty and delicious bread is excellent with a creamy potato soup or as a starter with a few olives and a slice of Serrano ham. (Picture p. 121).

4 loaves
Ideal dough temperature 26°C.
4 round cake tins

15 g yeast	2 red chillies
500 g water (5 dl)	30 g chives
750 g strong wheat flour	10 g crushed garlic
100 g polenta	
50 g olive oil (1.5 dl)	150 g grated cheddar
20 g sea salt	cheese
200 g maize kernels	25 g butter for greasing

1. Dissolve the yeast in the water and pour the mixture over the flour and polenta. Knead on low speed for 3 minutes and add the oil. Add the salt after another 11 minutes and increase the speed. Knead for 6 minutes until very elastic. Test the dough for elasticity.
2. Add the maize kernels. Rinse and finely chop the chillies. Remove the seeds if you prefer a milder bread. I personally like the hotter version. Mix in the chillies.
3. Rinse the chives and cut into strips. Crush the garlic with a knife and add towards the end.

4. Mix gently and place the dough in a lightly oiled lidded plastic container and leave for 120 minutes, knock back after half the time.
5. Turn out on a floured work surface and divide into four pieces. Grease the tins with butter, shape balls and place them seam down in the tins.
6. Sprinkle with grated cheese and leave to rise for 75 minutes until doubled in size.
7. Preheat the oven with the stone or tray to 250°C.
8. Put the tins in the oven and spray generously with water.
9. Lower the temperature to 180°C after 5 minutes. Open the oven door after another 10 minutes to let some air in. Repeat twice during baking.
10. Bake for a total of 40 minutes.
11. Take out the breads, remove the tins and bake for another 5 minutes on a tray so they form a crust all round and do not go soft and spongy.
12. Cool on a wire rack.

Onion Bread

I have made onion bread for over twenty years, and it is wonderful if done properly. I made this bread for my master baker exam at the beginning of the 1980s. It was a favourite with the examination board. If you like, add 100 g smoked, diced ham. (Picture p. 146)

3 loaves
Ideal dough temperature 26°C.

500 g finely chopped shallots	KNEADING
50 g olive oil	25 g yeast
	500 g water (5 dl)
	200 g wholemeal flour, preferably stone ground
STARTER	750 g strong wheat flour, preferably stone ground
2 g yeast	50 g butter
100 g water (1 dl)	10 g chopped chives
150 strong wheat flour, preferably stone ground	25 g sea salt
4 g salt	

Continued on p. 145.

Blueberry Bread (p. 142).

STARTER

Dissolve the yeast in the water and pour the mixture over the flour. Knead on low speed for 10 minutes. Add the salt and increase the speed. Knead for another 5 minutes until elastic. Place the dough in a lightly oiled lidded plastic container and leave for 3 hours at room temperature.

Peel and chop the shallots. Fry in olive oil on low heat until transparent, leave to cool completely.

KNEADING

1. Dissolve the yeast in the water and pour over the flour and the prepared starter. Add the fried shallots and knead for 3 minutes on the lowest speed. Add butter and chives and knead for another 11 minutes. Add the salt, increase the speed and knead for 5 minutes until the dough is elastic.
2. Place the dough in a lightly oiled lidded plastic container and leave for 60 minutes. Knock back once during rising.
3. Turn out on a floured work surface and divide into three.
4. Make round, tight balls.
5. Take three round baskets and dust with coarse rye flour. Place the balls seam down in the baskets and sprinkle with rye flour. Cover with a tea-towel and leave to rise for 75 minutes until doubled in size. (If you are not using baskets, sprinkle flour on a tea-towel, place the breads on it, pull up the cloth between them and cover).
6. Preheat the oven with the stone or tray to 250°C.
7. Place the breads in the oven and spray generously with water.
8. Lower the temperature to 200°C after 5 minutes. Open the oven door after another 10 minutes to let some air in. Repeat twice during baking.
9. Bake for a total of 50 minutes.
10. Take out the breads and place on a wire rack. Spray with water for a nicely crackled crust.

Suitable for freezing in plastic bags. Reheat in the oven and they will taste as good as fresh.

Fennel Bread

Fennel bread is moist and delicious. Study the text on baking with levain before you start.
(Picture p. 147)

4 loaves

1 batch White Bread with Levain dough, see p. 67.

400 g fennel	10 g finely ground dried
50 g olive oil (0.5 dl)	fennel
sea salt	50 g air-cured Italian ham
freshly ground white pepper	or coppa sausage

1. Rinse the fennel and cut into fine strips using a sharp knife.
2. Pour the oil into a small saucepan and fry the fennal at low temperature until it begins to get transparent and soft. Season with salt, white pepper and ground, dried fennel. Leave to cool.
3. Dice the ham and mix with the fennel strips.
4. Mix and knead the dough as in point 1 for White Bread with Levain. Mix in the ham and fennel. Place the dough in a lightly oiled lidded plastic container and leave for 170 minutes.
5. Turn out on a floured work surface and cut into four.
6. Take a tea-towel and dust liberally with wheat flour.
7. Gently fold the dough into three and place seam down on the towel. Cover with a tea-towel and leave to rise for 75 minutes until doubled in size.
8. Preheat the oven with the stone or tray to 250°C.
9. Turn over two of the breads seam up and put in the oven. Spray generously with water. Meanwhile, store the remaining two breads in the fridge.
10. Lower the temperature to 200°C after 5 minutes. Open the oven door after another 10 minutes to let some air in. Repeat twice during baking.
11. Bake for a total of 50 minutes.
12. Take out the breads and place on a wire rack. Spray with water for a nicely crackled crust.

Onion Bread (p. 143).

Fennel Bread (p. 145) ·

Tomato Bread (p. 150) and Olive Bread (p. 149).

Olive Bread

Use olives with stones, they taste better than the ones without. Remove the stones by beating them with your fist, if they are ripe the stones will come out easily. (Picture below and opposite)

4 loaves
Ideal dough temperature 24°C.

STARTER	400 g strong wheat flour,
2 g yeast	preferably stone ground
150 g water (1.5 dl)	2 g thyme
225 g strong wheat flour,	2 g finely ground aniseed
preferably stone ground	5 g oregano
6 g salt	50 g olive oil (0.5 dl)
	15 g sea salt
KNEADING	10 g crushed garlic
15 g yeast	
500 g water (5 dl)	350 g stoned black olives
25 g honey	
250 g coarse rye flour,	
preferably stone ground	
250 g durum wheat	

STARTER

Dissolve the yeast in the water and pour the mixture over the wheat flour. Knead the dough for 10 minutes on low speed. Add the salt and knead at a somewhat higher speed for another 5 minutes.

Place the dough in a lightly oiled lidded plastic container and leave for 3 hours at room temperature or over night in the fridge.

KNEADING

1. Dissolve the yeast in the water and pour over the starter and honey. Add flour, spices and herbs and knead for 3 minutes. Add the oil and knead on low speed for another 11 minutes. Add the salt, increase the speed somewhat and knead for 7 minutes until elastic.
2. Test the dough for elasticity. Add thet garlic towards the end.
3. Mix in the olives. Sprinkle 5 g of wheat flour over them for easier blending.
4. Place the dough in a lightly oiled lidded plastic container and leave for 60 minutes. Knock back once during rising.
5. Turn out on a floured work surface and divide into four.
6. Take four baskets and dust with fine rye flour.
7. Fold the dough and place seam down in the baskets. Sprinkle with rye flour and cover, or put on a floured teatowel, pulling the cloth up between the breads for support.
8. Leave to rise for approx. 75 minutes until doubled in size.
9. Preheat the oven with the stone or tray to 250°C.
10. Place the breads in the oven, two at the time, and spray generously with water. (Meanwhile, store the other two in the fridge.)
11. Lower the temperature to 200°C after 5 minutes. Open the oven door after another 10 minutes to let some air in. Repeat twice during baking.
12. Bake for a total of 45 minutes.
13. Take out the breads, place on a wire rack and spray with water for a nicely crackled crust.

Suitable for freezing in plastic bags.

Tip
Cut a thin slice, rub with a clove of garlic and roast in a hot skillet. Garnish with deseeded, chopped sun-dried tomatoes, chopped basil, shallots and season with flaky salt, coarsely ground black pepper and a dash of olive oil and you have a delicious bruschetta.

Tomato Bread

Tomato bread is a wonderful bread that goes well with salad, soup and Italian meats. (P. 148 and opposite.)

2 loaves
Ideal dough temperature 24°C.

STARTER	KNEADING
2 g yeast	20 g yeast
100 g water (1 dl)	500 g tinned crushed
150 g strong wheat flour,	tomatoes, premium
preferably stone ground	quality
4 g sea salt	650 g strong wheat flour,
	preferably stone ground
	150 g durum wheat
	50 g olive oil (0.5 dl)
	15 g sea salt
	2 g thyme
	5 g crushed garlic

STARTER

Dissolve the yeast in the water and pour over the flour in the bowl. Knead on the lowest speed for 13 minutes. Add the salt, increase the speed and knead for another 7 minutes until elastic. Place the dough in a lightly oiled lidded plastic container and leave to rise for 3 hours at room temperature or in the fridge overnight.

KNEADING

1. Dissolve the yeast in the tinned tomatos and pour over the starter and flour. Knead on the lowest speed for 3 minutes. Add the oil and work for another 11 minutes. Add salt and thyme.
2. Knead the dough for 7 minutes until elastic. Test for elasticity. Add the garlic towards the end.
3. Place the dough in a lightly oiled lidded plastic container and leave for 90–120 minutes, knock back the dough once.
4. Turn out on a floured work surface and divide in two.
5. Make two balls of dough, place in two round baskets dusted with flour and sprinkle flour on top. Cover and leave to rise for approx. 75 minutes until doubled in size or in the fridge overnight.
6. Preheat the oven with the stone or tray to 250°C.
7. Turn out one loaf at a time on a large spatula and slash a cross across the top. Place in the oven and spray generously with water.
8. Lower the temperature to 200°C after 5 minutes. Open the oven door after another 10 minutes to let some air in. Repeat twice during baking for a crispier result.
9. Take out the breads, place on a wire rack and spray with water for a nicely crackled crust.

Spinach Bread

This green-tinged bread with a nice spinachy flavour is very versatile. Use it as a sandwich base with a topping of smoked salmon and cold scrambled eggs, make rolls with crispy bacon or roasted sunflower seeds added to the dough. (Picture p. 141).

3 loaves
Ideal dough temperature 24°C.

STARTER	500 g spinach, defrosted
2 g yeast	and chopped
100 g water (1 dl)	650 g strong wheat flour,
150 g strong wheat flour,	preferably stone ground
preferably stone ground	150 g durum wheat
4 g sea salt	nutmeg, a pinch freshly
	grated
KNEADING	50 g olive oil (0.5 dl)
20 g yeast	15 g sea salt
100 g water (1 dl)	10 crushed garlic

STARTER

Dissolve the yeast in the water and pour over the flour in the bowl. Knead the dough on the lowest speed for 10 minutes. Add the salt, increase the speed somewhat and knead the dough for another 5 minutes until elastic. Place the dough in a lightly oiled lidded plastic container and leave for 3 hours at room temperature or in the fridge over night.

KNEADING

1. Dissolve the yeast in the water and spinach. Pour over the starter and add the flour. Add grated nutmeg and knead the dough on low speed for 3 minutes. Add the oil and keep kneading on low speed for 11 minutes.

Continued on p. 153.

Tomato Bread.

2. Add the salt and knead on higher speed for 7 minutes until elastic. Add the garlic during the final minute.
3. Place the dough in a lightly oiled lidded plastic container and leave for 90–120 minutes, knock back once during rising.
4. Turn out on a floured work surface.
5. Make three round balls and leave under a tea-towel for 5 minutes.
6. Roll out four points around the ball, brush with water and fold across the top.
7. Place on a floured tea-towel and leave to rise for approx. 90 minutes until doubled in size.
8. Preheat the oven with the stone or tray to 250ºC.
9. Place the breads in the oven using a spatula and spray generously with water.
10. Lower the temperature to 200ºC after 5 minutes. Open the oven door after another 10 minutes to let some air in. Repeat twice during baking.
11. Bake for a total of 45 minutes. Take out the breads and cool on a wire rack.

Spinach Bread with Smoked Salmon

This picnic bread goes very well with cucumber raita and sliced red onions. Moisten the bread with a little virgin olive oil. It should be eaten the same day and is not suitable for freezing.

3 loaves

1 batch Spinach Bread dough, see p. 150. Add 300 g chopped smoked salmon. Follow the recipe for Spinach Bread.

Spinach and Tomato Bread

4 loaves

This is the crescent moon shaped bread in the picture opposite. Make as follows:

1 batch Spinach Bread dough and follow the recipe for Tomat Bread dough, see p. 150.

1. Divide each dough into four equal pieces, make round balls, cover with a tea-towel and leave for 10 minutes. Place a tomato ball on top of a spinach ball and sprinkle with wheat flour. Roll out the middle so you get two "lips", one on either side. Fold them over and press down.
2. Place on a tea-towel dusted with flour, sprinkle with wheat flour, cover with a tea-towel and leave to rise for approx. 75 minutes or until doubled in size.
3. Slash with a sharp knife.
4. Bake as for Spinach Bread.

Spinach Bread with a Cap

4 loaves

Half a batch Tomato Bread dough and one batch Spinach Bread dough, see p. 150.

Caraway seeds

1. Turn out the doughs on a floured work surface. Divide each into four pices, make rolls, cover with a tea-towel and leave for 10 minutes. Place the spinach rolls on a tea-towel dusted with flour and pull up the cloth between the breads.
2. Roll out the tomato dough to make saucer shapes using a little wheat flour. Put them on top of the spinach ball and press down, brush the top with a little water and sprinkle with caraway seeds.
3. Cover with a tea-towel and leave to rise until doubled in size.
4. Preheat the oven with the stone or tray to 250ºC.
5. Place two of the breads in the oven and spray generously with water. Put the other two in the fridge.
6. Lower the temperature to 200ºC after 5 minutes. Open the oven door after another 10 minutes to let some air in. Repeat twice during baking.
7. Bake for a total of 45 minutes.
8. Take out the breads, place on a wire rack and spray with water for a nicely crackled crust.

These delicious breads are suitable for freezing in plastic bags. Heat in the oven and they will taste as good as new.

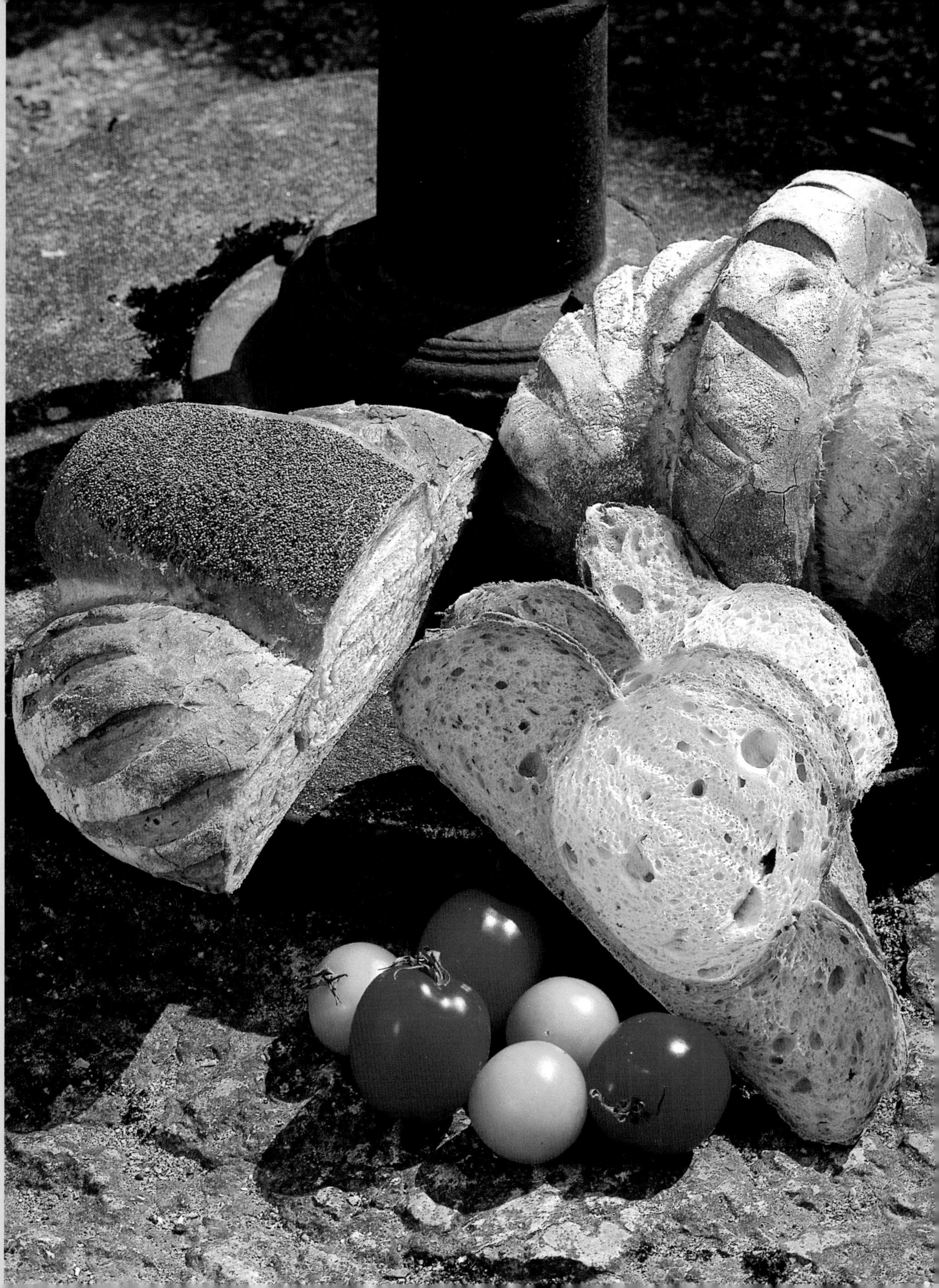

Variations of Tomato Dough and White Dough.

The Italian Flag

This bread is made up of three different doughs: one Italian panini dough, one tomato bread dough and one spinach bread dough. (See picture p. 152).

4 loaves

1 batch Spinach Bread dough, see p. 150
1 batch Tomato Bread dough, see p. 150

PANINI DOUGH
Ideal dough temperature 24°C

20 g yeast	800 g strong wheat flour
500 g water (5 dl)	salt
10 g set honey	
100 g fine rye flour, preferably stone ground	

Follow the instructions for Spinach Bread dough and Tomato Bread dough.

PANINI DOUGH

1. Dissolve the yeast in the water, add honey, rye flour and half the wheat flour. Stir with the spatula attachment until you get a frothy liquid, 5 minutes.
2. Cover with cling-film and leave for 30 minutes.
3. Switch to the dough hooks and add the remaining white flour. Knead the dough on low speed for 13 minutes. Add the salt and knead for another 7 minutes until very elastic.
4. Place the dough in a lightly oiled lidded plastic container and leave for 90 minutes, knock back once during rising.
5. Turn out on a floured work surface.

Divide each dough into four pieces. Make round balls, cover with a tea-towel and leave for 10 minutes. Begin with a spinach ball, put a panini ball on top and finally a tomato ball. Press a rolling pin across the centre of bread pile. Place on a tea-towel dusted with flour and sprinkle with plain flour. Cover with a towel and leave to rise for 75 minutes until doubled in size.

Bake as for Spinach Bread, see p. 150.

Variation of Tomato Dough and White Dough.

SPECIAL BREADS

Bagels (p. 174), Pretzels (p. 175) and Muffins (p. 159); top right, San Francisco Sourdough Bread with Levain (p. 173).

Muffins

When I was working on the M/S Vistafjord cruise liner, we made lots of fluffy muffins. Great toasted with butter and jam. (Picture opposite).

approx. 25 muffins

20 g yeast	10 g baking powder
625 g water (6.25 dl)	10 g sugar
875 strong wheat flour,	10 g butter
preferably stone ground	15 g sea salt
	rice flour

1. Dissolve the yeast in the water and add all the ingredients except butter and salt. Knead the dough on the lowest speed for 2 minutes, add the butter and keep kneading on low speed for 11 minutes.
2. Add the salt and increase the speed. Knead for another 7 minutes. Test the dough for elasticity.
3. Place the dough in a lightly oiled lidded plastic container and leave for 60 minutes. Knock back after 30 minutes.
4. Divide into 75 g pieces and shape the muffins. Cover with a tea-towel and leave for 10 minutes.
5. Sprinkle two tea-towels and the muffins with rice flour. Leave to rise for 30 minutes. Place a baking tray on top and press to flatten the muffins.
6. Leave to rise for another 30 minutes.
7. Preheat the oven with the stone or tray to 300ºC and heat the tray for 10 minutes. Place the muffins on the tray and bake for 5 minutes. Take out the tray, turn the muffins over and bake for another 3–5 minutes. Place on a wire rack and cover with a tea-towel to keep them soft.
8. Split with a fork. Keep in a plastic bag.

Tip
Keep in the fridge and take out as many as you need.

Pause Bread

This Swiss bread was created at the Richemont college in Luzern in the 1960s, and it has always been one of my favourites. When I went to college in Switzerland at the beginning of the 1970s these breads were very popular energy boosters for the local school children. (Picture p. 81).

approx. 25 rolls
Ideal dough temperature 26ºC.

STARTER	KNEADING
400 g fine wholemeal flour	10 g yeast
10 g yeast	200 g water (2 dl)
300 g water (3 dl)	275 fine wholemeal flour
	preferably stone ground
FILLING	20 g set honey
100 rasins	18 g sea salt
100 g hazel nuts	

STARTER
Weigh the flour, dissolve the yeast in the water and pour over the flour. Knead for 10 minutes. Place the dough in a lightly oiled lidded plastic container and leave to rise for 90 minutes at room temperature.

FILLING
1. Soak the raisins in cold water for 30 minutes. Drain.
2. Preheat the oven to 200ºC.
3. Roast the nuts in the oven for approx. 10 minutes until golden brown, stirring occasionally.
4. Peel off the skins by rubbing them in a towel. Remove.

KNEADING
1. Dissolve the yeast in the water and pour over the starter. Add flour and honey and knead on low speed for 10 minutes. Add salt and knead for 8 minutes until elastic. Mix in the drained raisins and the coarsely chopped hazelnuts.
2. Place the dough in a lightly oiled lidded plastic container.
3. Leave for 60 minutes. Knock back after 30 minutes.
4. Turn out on a floured work surface and divide in two. Roll out and cut off 60 g pieces. Make round, evenly shaped rolls.

Continued on p. 160

5. Place on a floured tea-towel, cover and leave to rise for 30 minutes.
6. Press down the middle with a rolling pin and leave to rise for another 45 minutes, or until doubled in size.
7. Preheat the oven with the stone or tray to 250°C.
8. Place the rolls on the stone or tray using a spatula and spray generously with water.
9. Bake for approx. 8 minutes until golden brown.
10. Remove the rolls and cool on a wire rack.

Tip
Using only wholemeal flour produces a moist bread with a strong cereal flavour, which tastes especially good with salted butter and apricot jam.

Cheese Bread

Cheese is a classic topping, but adding cheese to the dough is also delicious. Use a good emmentaler with a classic Swiss farmer's loaf, or any strong, mature hard cheese, for example cheddar. (Picture p. 140)

2 loaves
Ideal dough temperature 26°C.

BAUERNBROT DOUGH
20 g yeast
200 g water (2 dl)
300 g full-fat milk (3 dl)
100 g rye sourdough, p.29
500 g strong wheat flour
80 g wholmeal flour, preferably stone ground
200 g coarse rye flour, preferably stone ground

150 g strong cheese
10 g caraway seeds, whole
15 g sea salt

TOPPING
100 g grated cheese

1. Dissolve the yeast in the water and milk. Add sourdough and pour over the flour, cheese and caraway seeds.
2. Knead on the lowest speed for 13 minutes. Add salt and knead on slightly higher speed for another 7 minutes until elastic. Test the dough for elasticity.
3. Place the dough in a lightly oiled lidded plastic container and leave for 90–120 minutes, knock back twice during rising.
4. Turn out on a floured work tip and shape two dough balls.
5. Place on a floured tea-towel, cover and leave to rise for 30 minutes.
6. Press a rolling pin across the centre to make four sections (see below) and sprinkle with cheese. Leave to rise for another 30 minutes.

7. Preheat the oven with the stone or tray to 250°C.
8. Place the loaves in the oven and spray generously with water.
9. Lower the temperature to 200°C after 5 minutes. Open the oven door after another 10 minutes to let some air in. Repeat twice during baking.
10. Bake for a total of 50 minutes.
11. Take out the loaves, place on a wire rack and spray with water for a nicely crackled crust. Cool.

Suitable for freezing in plastic bags and defrosting in the oven.

Bouillabaisse Bread

The first time I made this delicious bread was when I worked as a guest baker at the prestigious Prinsen restaurant in Stockholm. (Picture p. 162).

2 loaves of 750 g each or 30 rolls of 25 g each
Ideal dough temperature 26°C.

30 g yeast	2 g dried thyme, rubbed to
550 g water, 20°C (5.5 dl)	release the flavour
850 g strong wheat flour,	1.5 g saffron
preferably stone ground	100 g olive oil (1 dl)
150 g coarse rye flour,	30 g sea salt
preferably stone ground	1 large crushed garlic clove

1. Dissolve the yeast in the water
2. Weigh flour and herbs and pour in mixture.
3. Knead the dough for 2 minutes on the lowest speed. Add the oil and knead for 8 minutes. Add the salt and work for 10 minutes on a higher speed. Add the garlic. Test the dough for elasticity.
4. Place in a lightly oiled lidded plastic container and leave for 60 minutes. Knock back after 30 minutes.
5. Turn out on a floured work surface and shape two round loaves.
6. Take two round baskets, dust with flour and place the loaves seam up inside, dust with flour. Cover with a tea-towel and leave to rise for approx. 75 minutes until doubled in size.
7. Preheat the oven with the stone or tray to 250°C.
8. Turn over the loaves on a large spatula and slash with a sharp knife.
9. Move the loaves to the stone or tray in the oven. Spray generously with water.
10. Lower the temperature to 200°C after 5 minutes. Open the oven door after another 10 minutes to let some air in. Repeat twice during baking.
11. Bake for a total of 50 minutes.
12. Take out, place on a wire rack and spray with water for a nicely crackled crust.

Suitable for freezing in plastic bags.

Tip
Make rolls using the recipe for French Bread Rolls, p. 63.
Serve warm with tapenade, olives and a pastis.

Crayfish Bread

This bread goes well with crayfish – which are cooked with dill in Sweden – add hard cheese and accompany with iced schnapps.

2 loaves

Use the same dough as for Swiss Zopf, p. 65.

dill tops
1 egg and a little salt for glazing
chilli powder
dill seeds

1. Add 4 finely chopped dill tops to the dough.
2. Divide the dough into two pieces corresponding to 2/3 of the dough.
3. Divide the rest into two smaller pieces.
4. Make round balls and cover with a tea-towel, leave for 10 minutes.
5. Make the body from the larger pieces and place on two trays.
6. Make claws from the smaller pieces and cut them open with a knife.
7. Whisk egg and salt and glace the bread. Sprinkle with chilli powder and dill seeds.
8. Leave to rise and bake as for Zopf, but reduce the baking time by 5 minutes.
9. Cool on a wire rack. They are even nicer heated before serving.

Bouillabaisse Bread (p. 161).

Crayfish Bread (p. 161).

Carrot Bread

This attractive, crackled bread tastes wonderful with soups or salads. (Picture p. 108).
Make your own carrot juice or buy ready made.

3 loaves
Ideal dough temperature 24°C.

DAY 1
POOLISH
5 g yeast
250 g water (2.5) dl
250 g coarse rye flour,
  preferably stone ground

DAY 2
KNEADING
50 g roasted sesame seeds
100 g roasted sunflower seeds
15 g yeast
250 g carrot juice, fresh
  (2.5 dl)
100 g grated carrot
20 g chopped parsley

650 g strong wheat flour,
  preferably stone ground
50 g set honey
50 g sunflower oil (0.5 dl)
20 g salt

CRACKLE GLAZING
6 g yeast
125 g rice flour
8 g sugar
8 g oil
3 g sea salt

DAG 1
POOLISH
Dissolve the yeast in the water and add the flour, whisk until the batter is smooth. Cover with cling-film and leave at room temperature overnight, 24 hours.

DAG 2
CRACKLE GLAZING
Dissolve the yeast in the water and add the remaining ingredients while you keep whisking. Cover with cling-film and leave for 30 minutes.

KNEADING
Preheat the oven to 200°C, roast the sesame seeds and then the sunflower seeds until golden brown.

1. Dissolve the yeast in the carrot juice, add grated carrot and parsley. Weigh flour and honey in the mixing bowl and add the poolish. Knead on low speed for 3 minutes.
2. Add the oil and knead for another 8 minutes. Add the salt and increase the speed, knead for 7 minutes until elastic.
3. Gently mix in the toasted seeds.
4. Place the dough in a lightly oiled lidded plastic container and leave for 60–90 minutes. Knock back after half the time.
5. Turn out on a floured work surface and divide into three.
6. Make three round balls of dough and cover with a tea-towel. Leave for 10 minutes.
7. Shape oblong loaves and place them on a tea-towel dusted with flour. Glaze generously with tiger glazing and leave to rise for 60–75 minutes or until doubled in size and the surface is crackled.
8. Preheat the oven with the stone or tray to 250°C.
9. Place the loaves in the oven and spray generously with water.
10. Lower the temperature to 200°C after 5 minutes. Open the oven door after another 10 minutes to let some air in. Repeat twice during baking.
11. Bake for a total of 45 minutes.
12. Take out the bread and cool on a wire rack. Do not spray with water, it will ruin the surface.

Camels' Tongues

This Persian bread should be the same length as the baking tray. Serve it warm with Middle-eastern food. (Picture p. 166).

4 loaves

1 egg for glazing
salt
25 g sesame seeds

1 batch Pita Bread dough, see p. 165

1. Divide the dough into four and make round balls.
2. Cover with a towel and leave for 5 minutes.
3. Roll out strands the same length as the tray using a little wheat flour. Place two on each tray.
4. Whisk the egg and a pinch of salt. Glaze.
5. Prick with a fork and sprinkle with sesame seeds.
6. Leave to rise for approx. 60 minutes until doubled in size in the unheated oven. Take out the loaves.

7. Preheat the oven to 250°C.
8. Place the loaves in the oven and spray generously with water. Bake for 8–10 minutes until golden brown.
9. Cool on the tray.

Suitable for freezing in plastic bags.

Sahara Bread

This Arab bread get their soft texture from the olive oil. They should be baked in a very hot oven to prevent them from drying out. Brush with water and sprinkle with sesame seeds.

4 flat breads

500 g strong wheat flour	550 g water (5.5 dl)
500 g white dinkel flour	15 g sea salt
20 g yeast	50 g olive oil (0.5 dl)

1. Weigh half of the flour (500 g) in the bowl. Dissolve the yeast in the water and add. Knead for 2 minutes on the lowest speed and 8 on high speed.
2. Add the remaining flour (500 g) and salt. Knead on the lowest speed for 8 minutes. Increase the speed and knead for 2 minutes until the dough no longer sticks to the side of the bowl. Add the olive oil.
3. Place the dough in a lightly oiled lidded plastic container and leave for 90 minutes.
4. Turn out on a floured work surface and divide into four equally-sized pieces. Make round balls and cover with a towel. Leave for 10 minutes.
5. Roll out round, flat cakes the size of a dinner plate and leave to rise on towels dusted with flour. Sprinkle with flour and cover. Leave for 30 minutes.
6. Preheat the oven with the stone or tray to 275°C.
7. Place the bread directly on the stone or tray in the oven and spray sparingly with water. Bake for approx. 8–10 minutes until golden brown.
8. Cool on a wire rack.

Tip
Serve warm with Arabic type food. Heat in a plastic bag at 75°C to prevent them from drying out. Suitable for freezing.

Pita Bread

For a light pita bread with a cavity that you can stuff with all kinds of delicacies you need a very elastic dough. It must be made with strong flour and a little olive oil to lubricate the gluten. Here follows a recipe that never fails. (Picture p. 166).

approx. 20 80 g breads
Ideal dough temperature 26°C.

30 g yeast	50 g olive oil (0.5 dl)
500 g water, 20°C (5 dl)	15 g sea salt
900 g strong wheat flour, preferably stone ground	

1. Dissolve the yeast in the water and add the wheat flour. Knead for 2 minutes on the lowest speed. Add the oil and knead for another 11 minutes. Add the salt, increase the speed and knead for 7 minutes. Test the dough for elasticity.
2. Place the dough in a lightly oiled lidded plastic container and leave for 60 minutes. Knock back after 30 minutes. It is very important that you work the dough well for a successful result.
3. Turn out on a floured work surface and divide in two. Roll out two long strands and cut off 100 g pieces, use scales for the correct weight.
4. Make dough balls, cover with a tea-towel and leave for 10 minutes.
5. Roll out the balls in wheat flour to the size of a small saucer.
6. Place on a tea-towel dusted with flour, cover and leave to rise for 45 minutes until doubled in size.
7. Preheat the oven with the stone or tray to 300°C.
8. Place the bread on the stone or tray. Spray with water.
9. Bake for approx. 5 minutes until golden brown and puffed up. Cool on a wire rack.

Top, decorative bread with bunch of grapes (p. 223) and The Lady (p. 223); bottom, Pita Bread (p. 165) Camels' Tongues (p. 164).

Naan Bread (p. 170).

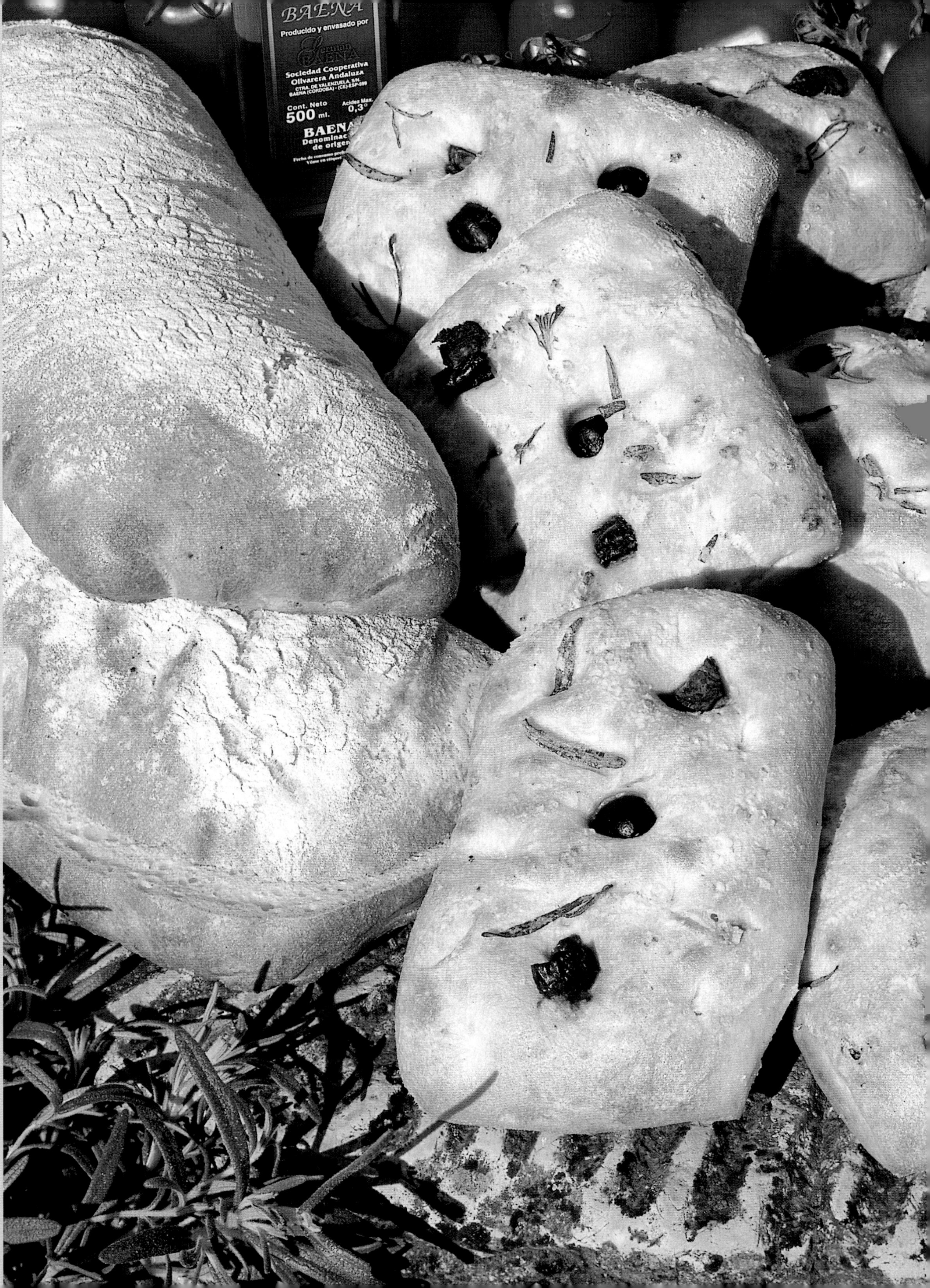

Ciabatta (p.171) and Focaccia (p. 170).

Fougasse (p. 172).

Naan Bread

I ate naan for the first time on a visit to my friends Anna and Erik in Islington, London. (Picture p. 167).

approx. 15 naan

STARTER	KNEADING
2 g yeast	900 g strong wheat flour
150 g full-fat milk (1.5 dl)	50 g sunflower oil (0.5 dl)
200 g wholemeal flour	10 g baking powder
	15 g honey
	30 g yeast
	500 g full-fat milk (5 d l)
	25 g salt

STARTER

Dissolve the yeast in the milk and add to the wholemeal flour. Knead on low speed for 10 minutes. Place in a lightly oiled lidded plastic container and leave for 3 hours.

KNEADING

1. Weigh flour, oil, baking powder and honey in a baking bowl. Add the starter. Dissolve the yeast in the milk and pour over the rest.
2. Knead for 10 minutes on the lowest speed and add salt. Increase the speed and knead for 8 minutes until very elastic. Test the dough for elasticity.
3. Place the dough in a lightly oiled lidded plastic container and leave for 60 minutes. Knock back after 30 minutes and again towards the end.
4. Turn out on a floured work surface and divide in two. Roll out two long strands. Cut off 120 g pieces and make round balls. Place on a tea-towel dusted with flour and cover. Leave for 10 minutes.
5. Roll out oval, flat breads using a little flour. Place on trays greased with oil, 6 on each. Sprinkle with wholemeal flour and cover with a tea-towel. Leave to rise for approx. 45 minutes in room temperature until doubled in size.
6. Preheat the oven to 275ºC.
7. Bake for approx. 5 minutes until golden brown. Take out the bread and wrap in a towel. Serve warm with Indian food.

Suitable for freezing. Heat before serving.

Focaccia

This Italian classic can be made in a tin and cut up into squares after baking. The bread should be light and fluffy, golden brown, smelling slightly of olive oil and topped with fresh rosemary or flaky salt. (Picture p. 168)

I sometimes make basil focaccia with sundried tomatoes by mixing the water with 50 g of basil, adding a topping of sun-dried tomatoes, slices of parmesan or pine nuts.

approx. 21 squares
Ideal dough temperature 24ºC.

35 yeast		GLAZING
500 g water (5 dl)		0.5 dl olive oil
5 g set honey		1 crushed garlic clove
500 g strong wheat flour,		
preferably stone ground		TOPPING
150 g durum sheat		40 black olives with stones
5 g oregano, dried		10 sun-dried tomatoes
50 g olive oil		1 pot fresh rosemary
15 g sea salt		flaky salt

1. Dissolve the yeast in the water and honey. Add to the flour and oregano. Knead on low speed for 3 minutes. Add oil and knead for another 10 minutes.
2. Add the salt, increase the speed and work on high speed until the dough stops sticking to the sides of the bowl, approx. 7 minutes.
3. Grease a low-edged tin with olive oil and place the dough in it. Glaze the top with olive oil and cover with cling-film. Leave to rise for 90–120 minutes.
4. Turn out on a floured work surface and divide into three equel lengths. Cut each into seven pieces.
5. Move to a tray. Make indentations with your fingers and glaze with olive oil and garlic. Press two olives and two pieces of sun-dried tomato on top and sprinkle with fresh rosemary and salt.
6. Preheat the oven to 250ºC.
7. Place the tray in the oven and spray generously with water.
8. Bake for approx. 8 minutes until golden brown.
9. Take out the bread and cool on a wire rack.

Suitable for freezing in plastic bags and warming up in the oven.

Ciabatta

This Italian bread resembling a slipper comes in a variety of versions. Genuine ciabatta should be light and fluffy inside with large holes. This is achieved by using a starter, or poolish, and leaving overnight at room temperature. To get the large holes the dough needs to be loose.
(Picture p. 168)

4 loaves
Ideal dough temperature 24ºC.

DAY 1	DAY 2
POOLISH	KNEADING
2 g yeast	5 g yeast
250 g water (2.5 dl)	250 g water (2.5 dl)
250 g strong wheat flour, preferably stone ground	250 g durum wheat
	125 g strong wheat flour, preferably stone ground
	15 g sea salt
	olive oil

DAY 1

POOLISH

Dissolve the yeast in the water and whisk down the flour until you have a thick batter.
Cover with cling-film and leave at room temperature for 24–48 hours.

DAY 2

KNEADING

1. Dissolve the yeast in the water. Add to the flour, add poolish. Knead on low speed for 13 minutes.
2. Add salt and knead for 7 minutes until the dough is elastic and does not stick to the sides of the bowl.
3. Grease a low-edged baking tin with olive oil and put the dough in the tin. Sprinkle with olive oil and distribute over the bottom of the tin.
4. Leave to rise for 60–90 minutes.
5. Sift durum wheat on to the work surface and turn out the dough. Preheat the oven with the stone or tray to 250ºC.
6. Divide the dough into four and place in the oven Spray generously with water.
7. Bake for 25 minutes. Lower the temperature to 200ºC after 5 minutes. Open the oven door after another 10 minutes to let some air in.
8. Cool on a wire rack.

Tomato ciabattas
Use tomato juice instead of water.

Olive ciabattas with rosemary
Add 200 g pitted olives and fresh rosemary at the end of kneading.

Ciabatta bigia
Exchange 100 g of the wheat flour during the kneading for rye flour, add 200 g pitted black olives and 25 g chopped basil. Sprinkle with rye instead of durum flour.

Tip
All ciabattas freeze very well in plastic bags and can be warmed up in the oven.

Ciabatta Café de Paris
When I attended the international sugar craft school in Zurich, we often spent the evening at a Mövenpick restaurant where we had Ciabatta Café de Paris with a mixed salad. Accompanied by a beer it was a great and inexpensive meal that suited our slender wallets.

Café de Paris butter is often used for entrecote or snails, a Swiss restaurant classic.

BUTTER CAFÉ DE PARIS	
150 g shallots	10 g lemon juice (2 tsp)
1 large garlic clove	15 g brandy (1tbsp)
15 g olive oil (1 tbsp)	15 g Madeira (tbsp)
1 g dried thyme	5 g Worcestershire sauce (1tsp)
1 g dried marjoram	5 g Dijon mustard, yellow
1 g dried rosemary	5 g tomato puré
4.5 g dried tarragon	15 g fresh parsely
3 g rose paprika	5 g fresh chives
3 g sea salt	2 anchovies
3 g hot curry powder	
2.5 g white pepper	675 g butter
15 g Aromat flavour enhancer	100 g egg (2 eggs)

1. Peel and finely chop the shallots and crush the garlic. Fry gently in oil on low heat until the onion is transparent and yellow.
2. Put the onions in a mixer. Add the dry spices (weighed on a letter balance) and the wet ingredients. Add the chopped parsley, chives and anchovies. Mix until fluffy. Cover with a lid and leave at room temperature until the next day.
3. Whisk the soft butter until fluffy. Add the herb mix and eggs and whisk until light and fluffy.

Continued on p. 172

4. Cut the ciabatta lengthways and spread generously with the butter. Toast in the oven until golden brown at 275°C. Delicious with a crisp salad.

Keeps for a long time in an air-tight container in the fridge or freezer.

Fougasse

This bread from southern France evokes Nice and the Boulevard des Anglais, which meanders past the elegant Hotel Negresco. (Picture p. 169)

4 breads
Ideal dough temperature 26°C.

700 g strong wheat flour, preferably stone ground	75 g Italian salami, air-cured Italian or Spanish ham, diced.
100 fine rye flour, preferably stone ground	
100 g wholemeal flour, preferably stone ground	75 g olive oil and 2 garlic cloves crushed with a pestle and mortar for topping
15 g herbes de Provence mixed herbs	
20 g yeast	
650 g water (6.5 dl)	flaky salt, fresh rosemary, oregano and thyme for decoration
50 g olive oil (0.5 dl)	
20 g sea salt	

1. Weigh the dry ingredients and spices.
2. Dissolve the yeast in the water and pour over the flour. Add the herbs.
3. Knead on low speed for 3 minutes. Add the oil and knead for another 10 minutes. Add the salt, increase speed and knead for 8 minutes until very elastic.
4. Check for elasticity and mix in salami or ham. Test the dough for elasticity. Place the dough in a lightly oiled lidded plastic container and leave for 60 minutes. Knock back after 30 minutes.
5. Divide the dough into four pieces and make four evenly-shaped balls, cover with a tea-towel and leave for 5 minutes.
6. Roll out into flat ovals, slightly larger than a dinner plate. Place on two greased trays or use a tea-towel. Make a few cuts and pull a little to open up (see picture p. 169). Make indentations with your fingers. Brush with olive oil and garlic. Sprinkle with mixed

herbs, e.g. fresh rosemary, thyme and oregano, and some flaky salt, or, if you prefer, just one of these.
7. Leave to rise until doubled in size on a tray, approx. 45 minutes.
8. Preheat the oven to 250°C.
9. Bake for 12–15 minutes until golden brown and repeat with the remaining two.
10. Cool on a wire rack.

Freeze in plastic bags and heat in the oven.

Rieska

I got this recipe, originating in Lappland and eastern Finland, from Seppo Peltimäki, a colleague in Turkku. (Picture p. 176)

4 breads
Ideal dough temperature 28°C.

50 g yeast	200 g strong wheat flour, preferably stone ground
500 g water (5 dl)	
125 g oatmeal	15 g golden syrup
300 g barley flour	20 g sea salt

1. Dissolve the yeast in the water and pour over the other ingredients. Knead for 10 minutes on the lowest speed. Increase the speed and knead for 2 minutes. Cover and leave for 45 minutes.
2. Divide the dough into four pieces of 300 g each, make round balls, cover with a tea-towel and leave for 5 minutes. Shape round flat cakes, approx. 8 mm thick, using barley flour. Prick with a fork.
3. Place on two trays covered with baking sheets, cover and leave to rise for about 45 minutes until doubled in size.
4. Preheat the oven to 250°C and bake for 12 minutes until light brown.
5. Cool on a wire rack.

Tip
Do not leave too long in the oven or the bread gets too dry. The texture should be light.
Serve with smoked salmon, potato salad with dill and a little whitefish roe with chopped red onion and chives.

San Francisco Sourdough Bread

Ever since the days of the gold rush, San Francisco has been famous for its delicious sourdough bread. Real sourdough bread is made from wild yeast and mostly plain flour. A classic Frisco variation is based on sourdough made with yoghurt; but a tangy, white levain has the same effect. (See Baking with Levain, p. 30).

This wonderful bread should be well kneaded with a thick crust and a light and fluffy interior with large holes. (Picture p. 158).

2 loaves
Ideal dough temperature 24ºC.

POOLISH
500 g water (5 dl)
400 g strong wheat flour,
    preferably stone ground
400 g levain, see p. 31

KNEADING
400 g strong wheat flour,
    preferably stone ground
20 g sea salt

POOLISH
1. Whisk together the ingredients for the poolish to a smooth, thick batter with a hand whisk. Cover with a tea-towel and leave at room temperature for 4–5 hours. By this time it should be active and bubbly with a sour smell.

KNEADING
2. Pour the poolish into the mixing bowl and add half the wheat flour. Work on low speed for 2 minutes. Increase the speed and knead for 8 minutes.
3. Change to the dough hooks and add the remaining flour and salt. Knead on low speed for 8 minutes, increase the speed and knead for 2 minutes until the dough no longer sticks to the side of the bowl. It should be very elastic.
4. Place the dough in a lightly oiled lidded plastic container and leave for 60 minutes.
5. Turn out on a floured work surface, fold over in the shape of a pillow. Knock back well and replace in the box. Repeat twice. Total rising time 3 hours.
6. Turn out on to a floured work surface and divide in two. Fold to make two long loaves without pressing the air out of the dough. Place in two baskets dusted with flour or leave to rise on a tea-towel dusted with flour, sprinkle with flour and cover.
7. Leave to rise in a warm place until doubled in size, approx. 3–4 hours, or overnight, in the baskets.

8. Preheat the oven with the stone or tray to 250ºC.
9. Place the bread in the oven and spray generously with water.
10. Lower the temperature to 180ºC after 10 minutes. Open the oven door a few time during baking.
11. Bake for a total of approx. 50 minutes. The bread should be fairly dark. If not, the crust gets chewy.
12. Rermove from the oven and cool on a wire rack. Spray with water.

Tip
Suitable for freezing, but after working a whole day with this wonderful bread you should eat it the same day. Serve with crab or fish soup.

Beer Bread

This beer bread has a rustic look and tastes different depending on what kind of beer you are using. I have used Guinness, but a well-flavoured lager works just as well. (Picture p. 177)

4 loaves
Ideal dough temperature 26ºC.

STARTER
2 g yeast
150 g water (1.5 dl)
200 g strong wheat flour
5 g salt

KNEADING
15 g yeast
250 g water (2.5 dl)
250 g Guinness (2.5 dl)
100 fine rye flour, preferably stone ground
100 g wholemeal flour, preferably stone ground

550 g strong wheat flour, preferably stone ground
175 g durum wheat
25 g set honey
50 g olive oil (0.5 dl)
20 g salt

BEER TOPPING
10 g yeast
250 g Guinness (2.5 dl)
5 g sea salt
250 g coarse rye flour, preferably stone ground

BEER TOPPING
Dissolve the yeast in the beer using a whisk. Add the salt and flour and whisk until you have a smooth batter. Leave to rise covered with cling-film 30 minutes before use.

Continued on p. 174

STARTER

Dissolve the yeast in the water. Pour over the wheat flour and knead on the lowest speed for 10 minutes until elastic. Add the salt and knead for another 5 minutes. Place the dough in a lightly oiled lidded plastic container and leave to rise at room temperature for 3 hours or in the fridge overnight.

KNEADING

1. Dissolve the yeast in the water and beer. Pour over the starter, flour and honey.
2. Knead for 3 minutes. Add the oil and work for another 5 minutes. Add the salt, increase the speed and kneed for 8 minutes until elastic. Test the dough for elasticity.
3. Place the dough in a lightly oiled lidded plastic container and leave for 60 minutes. Knock back after half the time.
4. Turn out on a floured work surface and divide into four pieces. Fold in three.
5. Glaze with the beer topping and sprinkle generously with rye flour.
6. Leave to rise on a tea-towel dusted with flour for approx. 45 until doubled in size.
7. Preheat the oven with the stone or tray to 250°C.
8. Place the bread in the oven and spray generously with water.
9. Lower the temperature to 200°C after 5 minutes. Open the oven door after another 10 minutes to let some air in. Repeat twice during baking.
10. Bake for a total of 50 minutes.
11. Take out the bread and cool on a wire rack.

Bagels

Bagels with cream cheese, smoked salmon and red onions is a New York classic, a Jewish specialty with roots in Eastern Europe. Bagels are boiled before they are baked in the oven. A perfect bagel is golden brown and has a dense, chewy texture. (Picture p. 158)

You can twist it like a pretzel if you like, glaze it with egg and dip it in caraway seeds and a little flaky salt. Very nice with German sausage, mustard and sauerkraut.

approx. 25 bagels
Ideal dough temperature 26°C.

STARTER	
20 g yeast	50 g sunflower oil (0.5 dl) or butter
250 g water, 20°C (2.5 dl)	25 g salt
375 g strong wheat flour, preferably stone ground	
	50 g set honey for boiling
KNEADING	2 eggs and a pinch of salt for glazing
25 g yeast	sesame seeds, poppy seeds or mature, grated cheese
250 g full-fat milk (2.5 dl)	
750 g strong wheat flour, preferably stone ground	
10 g set honey	

STARTER

Dissolve the yeast in the water. Add to the flour in the bowl. Knead on the lowest speed for 10 minutes. Place in a lightly oiled lidded plastic container and leave to rise for 3 hours at room temperature or overnight in the fridge.

KNEADING

1. Dissolve the yeast in the milk and add to the starter. Add the other ingredienses except salt and oil/butter.
2. Knead for 3 minutes on low speed and add oil or butter. Knead for 5 minutes and add salt. Increase the speed and knead for 10 minutes until very elastic. Test the dough for elasticity.
3. Place in a lightly oiled lidded plastic container and leave for 30 minutes.
4. Turn out on a floured work top and divide in two. Cut off 60 g pieces and make small oblong shapes.
5. Cover with a tea-towel and leave for 5 minutes. Roll out 30 cm pieces and make rings. Seal firmly so they do not come undone during rising.
6. Place on a tea-towel lightly dusted with flour. Cover

and leave to rise until doubled in size, approx 45 minutes.

7. Bring 5 l of water with 50 g honey to the boil. Gently lower the dough rings into the simmering water and poach for about 1 minute. Turn over a couple of times. Remove with a slotted spoon and drain on a wire rack.
8. Preheat the oven to 230ºC.
9. Place the bagels on a greased tin, glaze with egg and salt and dip in poppy seeds, sesame seeds or strong, mature grated cheese.
10. Bake for 12–15 minutes until golden brown.
11. Cool on a wire rack.

Wholemeal bagels
Exchange 250 g of the plain flour for wholemeal flour.

Rye sourdough bagels
Exchange 250 g of the wheat flour for rye flour, add 150 g sourdough made with rye flour (see p. 29) and reduce the amount of milk by 100 g.

Cinnamon and raisin bagels
Add 100 g demerara sugar, 10 g ground cinnamon and 100 g raisins that have been soaked in 10 g dark rum. Glaze with melted butter and dip in sugar mixed with cinnamon powder after baking.

Suitable for freezing. Defrost and warm briefly in the oven and they will be as good as new.

Beer Pretzel, Salt Pretzel

The October beer festival in Munich is a haven for this thirst-inducing bread. This classic twisted bread originates in southern Europe, and over the centuries it has changed shape many times. Sailors call them caustic soda rolls since they are dipped in a mixture of caustic soda and water before baking. (Picture pp. 158 and 177)

Note. *Caustic soda is corrosive, so make sure you do not come into contact with the solution. Fortunately, this is the only bread in this book for which you need protective clothing. Use rubber gloves and protective glasses and you will be safe.*

approx. 25 pretzels

Use the same dough as for bagels, see p. 174, but use butter instead of oil.

CAUSTIC SODA SOLUTION
100 g caustic soda
2,000 g water (2 litres)
Place the soda in a stainless steel saucepan, add half the water and bring to the boil. Add the rest of the cold water.

Twists
Shape two long ropes. Cut off 60–80 g pieces. Make oblong shapes, cover with a tea-towel and leave for 5 minutes. Roll out 45–50 cm strips, somewhat thicker in the centre. Twist into a pretzel shape and place on a tea-towel. Cover and leave to rise until doubled in size, approx. 45 minutes.

Délices
Cut off 60 g pieces, make round balls and cover with a tea-towel. Leave for 5 minutes. Roll out triangles using a little wheat flour. Make crescent shapes, place on a tea-towel and leave to rise like twists.

Oblong and round délices
Cut 60 g pieces, shape balls and oblong rolls and leave to rise as for the other types.

1. Preheat the oven to 230ºC.
2. Check that the temperature of the solution is 40ºC.
3. Put on the rubber gloves and a pair of protective glasses before dipping the bread in the solution.
4. Place on a greased baking tray.
5. Make a couple of slashes with a sharp knife and sprinkle with a little flaky salt.
6. If you are making délices, make a deep slash in the centre and sprinkle with flaky salt after dipping. Both shapes are slashed three times.
7. Bake for approx. 12–15 minutes until golden brown.
8. Cool on a wire rack.

Suitable for freezing in plastic bags. Defrost for 5 minutes in 200ºC.

Tip
Pretzels go very well with beer and Rohschinken, salami, bresaola and coppa, or cheese, radishes and gherkins.

Rieska (p. 172), Rolf's Bread (p. 204).

Grissini Bread Sticks

Grissini should be light, crisp and served as an appetizer before dinner or make you thirsty for beer. (Picture p. 177)

1 batch bagel dough, see p. 174

1. Roll out the dough and divide into 75 g pieces. Roll out sticks the length of the width of the baking tray. Place on a greased tray.
2. Glaze with beaten egg (with a pinch of salt) and sprinkle with flaky salt. Leave to rise for 30 minutes.
3. Place in the oven heated to 230°C and bake for 10 minutes until golden brown.

Beetroot Grissini

1. Proceed as above, but replace the dough with beetroot dough, see p. 123.
2. Glaze with egg and sprinkle with flaky salt and caraway seeds. Bake as Grissini.

Tip
The grissini dough can of course be flavoured with e.g. paprika, chilli or curry powder, finely chopped dill or parsley. Why not add finely diced smoked ham or salami and sprinkle with grated cheese instead of salt.

Store in a dry place for crispness.

Pizza

When I set out to write this book I was not going to include pizza, but I changed my mind. A good bread book should include a good pizza dough, so here is my version. The pizzas get even better if you bake them on a stone or hot baking tray.

4 pizzas

POOLISH	KNEADING
75 g water (0.75 dl), 28°C	325 g strong wheat flour, preferably stone ground
25 g yeast	
75 g strong wheat flour, preferably stone ground	175 g water (1.75 dl)
	10 g sea salt

POOLISH
1. Make sure the water is 28°. Dissolve the yeast in the water and whisk in the flour to make a smooth batter.
2. Cover with cling-film and leave to rise for 60 minutes at room temperature.

KNEADING
3. Place flour and water in a bowl. Add poolish and knead on the lowest speed for 13 minutes.
4. Add the salt, increase the speed and knead for another 7 minutes until elastic.
5. Turn out on a floured work surface and divide into four equl pieces. Make round, tight balls. Cover with a tea-towel and leave to rise until doubled in size for approx. 2 hours.
6. Flatten the pieces with your hand and roll out thin. Press down with your knuckles 2 cm inside the rim for the classic raised edge.
7. Make classic pizzas such as Calzone, Margerita, Napoli and Frutti di mare straight on the stone or tray at 250°C until they are golden brown and the base is baked.

Tip
You now have a useful dough, which you can cover in crushed, drained tomatoes. Add your favourite toppings, e.g. add thin slices of mozzarella on top and a few dashes of olive oil before it goes in the oven. A real Italian pizza base should be crisp, not tough and chewy.

SCALDED BREADS FROM THE SOUTH OF SWEDEN

Laputa Bread

This bread from the city of Malmö is a scalded, light and fluffy bread that is perfect for making sandwiches and keeps well.

4 loaves
Ideal dough temperature 26°C.

DAY 1
SCALDING 1
250 g fine rye flour,
   preferably stone ground
30 g sea salt
500 g water (5 dl)

DAY 2
SCALDING 2
50 g yeast
125 g water (1.25 dl)
400 g fine rye flour/wheat
   flour mix

KNEADING
600 g fine rye flour/wheat
   flour mix
600 g strong wheat flour,
   preferably stone ground
375 g water (3.75 dl)
150 sunflower oil (1.5 dl)
210 g golden syrup

50 g butter for glazing

DAY 1
SCALDING
Weigh flour and salt in a bowl. Bring the water to the boil in a saucepan and pour the boiling water over the flour. Knead until smooth with a ladle and cover with cling-film. Leave overnight.

DAY 2
SCALDING 2
Dissolve the yeast in the water, add flour and the scalded flour. Knead for 5 minutes. Cover with cling-film and leave to rise for 60 minutes.

KNEADING

1. Add the flours, water, oil and syrup for scalding 2. Knead on low speed for 15 minutes until elastic. Test the dough for elasticity. Do not work for too long.
2. Place the dough in a lightly oiled plastic container with a lid and leave for 60 minutes. Knock back after half the time.
3. Turn out on a floured work surface and divide into four equal pieces. Shape four round balls, cover with a tea-towel. Leave for 5 minutes.
4. Knock the balls into four, square breads. Grease a roasting pan with soft butter, glaze the breads with butter and place in the pan. Prick with a fork. Sprinkle with wheat flour.
5. Cover with a tea-towel and leave to rise until doubled in size for approx. 45 minutes.
6. Preheat the oven to 250°C.
7. Place the breads in the oven and spray with water.
8. Lower the temperature to 200°C after 5 minutes. Open the oven door after another 10 minutes to let some air in. Repeat twice during baking.
9. Bake for a total of 55–60 minutes. Use a thermometer to check if they are ready (98°C).
10. Take the pan out of the oven, separate the breads and cool on a wire rack.

Suitable for freezing in plastic bags.

Old-fashioned bread with aniseed and fennel seeds

4 loaves

This is a lovely, moist bread. Follow the instructions for Laputa bread, but mix in 10 g of ground aniseed and 10 g of ground fennel seeds at the scalding phase. Glaze with potato flour glazing, see p. 38.

Good, old-fashioned bread from the south of Sweden (p. 182), Laputa Bread (p. 182) and Sweet and Sour Bread (p. 185).

Sweet and Sour Bread

This slightly tangy bread is common in the southern provinces of Skåne and Halland. It was one of the basic breads served at home when I was a boy. It is made with scalded rye flour, which is common in Skåne. The result is a moist bread that goes well with smoked sausage or cheese. It is has a slightly sweet flavour since the starch in the flour turns into sugar overnight.

4 loaves
Ideal dough temperature 26°C.

DAY 1

SCALDING 1
250 fine rye flour,
   preferably stone ground,
or a mix of rye and plain
   wheat flour
25 g sea salt
10 g caraway seeds
500 g water (5 dl)

DAY 2

SCALDING 2
100 g fine rye flour,
   preferably stone ground
250 g strong wheat flour,
   preferably stone ground
   or unmixed rye and wheat
   flour
150 g sourdough based on
   rye flour, see p. 29
20 g yeast
100 g water (1 dl)

KNEADING
50 g yeast
500 g water (5 dl)
700 g strong wheat flour,
   preferably stone ground
200 g golden syrup

50 g butter for glazing

DAY 1

SCALDING 1
Weigh flour, salt and caraway seed in a bowl. Bring the water to the boil and pour over the flour. Mix until smooth in texture. Cover with cling-film and leave to mature over night.

DAY 2

SCALDING 2
Mix the scalded flour, flours and sourdough. Dissolve the yeast in the water with a whisk and pour over the flours. Knead on low speed for 5 minutes. turn out in a lightly oiled plastic box with a lid and leave to ferment for 3 hours.

KNEADING
1. Dissolve the yeast in the water, add scalding 2. Add wheat flour and syrup and knead for 15 minutes on low speed until elastic. Test the dough for elasticity.
2. Place the dough in a lightly oiled plastic container with a lid and leave for 45 minutes. Knock back after half the time. Turn out on a floured work top and divide into four equal pieces. Make four round buns. Cover with a tea-towel and leave for 5 minutes.
3. Grease a roasting pan with softened butter.
4. Make four square breads and glaze with the soft butter. Place in the pan and prick with a fork.
5. Leave to rise until doubled in size, 45–60 minutes.
6. Preheat the oven to 250°C.
7. Put the tray in the oven and spray with generous amounts of water.
8. Lower the temperature to 200°C after 5 minutes. Open the oven door after another 10 minutes to let some air in. Repeat twice during baking.
9. Bake for a total of 55–60 minutes. Check that they are ready using a thermometer (98°C).
10. Make a batch of potato flour glazing, see p. 38, and glaze the loaves while still warm. They will get too sticky if they are left to cool first.
11. Carefully remove the loaves from the pan and cool on a wire rack.

Scalded bread contains more water than other bread types, so it is especially important to use a thermometer to check that they are ready.

Suitable for freezing in plastic bags.

BRIOCHES, CROISSANTS

AND OTHER ENRICHED DOUGHS

Brioches

The name is said to derive from the French province of Brie. The brioche should have a strong buttery taste without being greasy. The secret is to make a very elastic dough before adding soft butter that has been left out at room temperature.

In France, it is customary to add between 500 and 750 g of butter per kilo of flour for a light and fluffy brioche. We used to have to work fast to prevent the buttery dough from getting sticky.

Typical for a first-class brioche is its light and fluffy interior, which is achieved by long rising times. You can never cheat with shorter rising times. (Picture p. 190).

20 small or 1 large brioche

BRIOCHE DOUGH	
20 g yeast	2 eggs and a pinch of salt for glazing
250 g egg (approx. 5)	50 g butter for greasing the small tins
500 g strong wheat flour, preferably stone ground	25 g butter for a large tin
20 g salt	
60 g sugar	
375 g unsalted butter	

DAY 1

1. Place the yeast in a bowl, add egg and whisk until the yeast has dissolved.
2. Add flour, salt and sugar. Knead for 15 minutes until elastic. Test the dough for elasticity.
3. Add the butter, a quarter of the amount at the time. Knead until shiny and smooth before adding the next batch of butter.
4. Place the dough in a lightly oiled plastic container with a lid and leave to rise until doubled in size at kitchen temperature, approx. 2 hours. Knock back the dough and knead with your hands until shiny.
5. Replace in the container and put in the fridge over night, min. 12 hours, max. 24 hours.

DAY 2

1. Turn out on a floured work surface and fold into a box shape.

2. *For small, individual brioches,* grease 20 brioche tins, divide the dough into 20 pieces and roll into balls. Shape a knob on top, 2/3 of the size of the ball. Place the ball into the tin, large ball down, or it will tip over in the oven.

For a large brioche, divide the dough into four equal parts and make round balls. Grease a large brioche tin, place three of the balls at the bottom and press down the fourth at the centre.

3. Glaze with beaten egg with a pinch of salt. Make sure the egg does not run down into the tin, otherwise the brioches will stick and not rise properly in the oven.
4. Leave to rise at room temperature or in the unheated oven until doubled in size, approx. 90 minutes for the large and 60 minutes for the small brioches.
5. Preheat the oven to 220°C and glaze the brioches with egg. Cut the large brioche six times with a pair of scissors, but not the small ones.
6. Bake until golden brown, the large for 45–50 minutes and the small for 8–9 minutes.
7. Immediately remove the tins and cool on a wire rack.

Brioche Nanterre

4 loaves

Take four 100 g pieces for each tin and make hot dog bread shapes. Place in rectangular, greased sponge cake tins and leave to rise as for regular brioche dough. Glaze with egg and slash the centre to prevent them from splitting (see p. 16). Bake for 35 minutes.

You can make rolls or plaits in order to sever the gluten strings. This will produce a softer bread than the one piece loaf where the strings run all the way along.

Suitable for freezing. Heat at 200°C and they will be as good as new.

Useful to know
It is possible to make a dough with a lot of butter due to the eggs. Eggs contain lecithin and can bind large amounts of butter without the dough getting greasy on the surface. Similar examples are hollandaise and béarnaise sauces and mayonnaise that all contain egg. One egg yolk can bind 2 dl of oil in mayonnaise.

Brioches (p. 188) and Croissants (p. 191).

Croissants

This French breakfast bread is said to originate from Budapest or Vienna. One thing is certain though – it was a French pastry-cook who, in 1920, first rolled butter into the dough, just as for pastry dough. Every day people came from far and wide to buy his flaky, fresh crossants.

16 croissants

20 g yeast	10 g salt
125 g water (1.25 dl)	300 g unsalted butter
150 g full-fat milk (1.5 dl)	
500 g strong wheat flour,	GLAZING
preferably stone ground	1 egg and a pinch of salt
55 g sugar	

DAY 1

1. Dissolve the yeast in the water in a 2 l bowl. Whisk in the milk
2. Pour flour, sugar and salt into the bowl and knead until the dough no longer sticks to the sides of the bowl, approx. 5 minutes.
3. Place the dough in a lightly oiled plastic container with a lid and leave to rise for 2 hours until doubled in size.
4. Knock back by quickly turning the dough over and pressing the air out of it. Replace in the container and leave overnight in the fridge, for a minimum of 8–12 hours. Check it for the first couple of hours since the dough may start to rise again, depending on the temperature inside your fridge. If it does, knock back again to prevent wild yeast forming.

DAY 2

1. Cut a cross in the top of the dough. Roll out in four places on a lightly floured work surface. Turn the dough 90° each time.
2. Soften the cold butter with the rolling pin and place in the centre of the dough. The butter should have the same texture as the dough to prevent the butter and dough from separating. Fold the four flaps across the dough and make sure that the butter is completely covered and cannot escape.
3. Dust the dough and work surface with flour. Roll out a rectangle, 40x70 cm. Roll from the centre towards the edge. Brush off the flour.
4. Fold in three. Wrap in cling-film and leave for 30 minutes in the fridge. Repeat the rolling-out process

twice. Leave for 30 minutes so that the tension in the dough does not destroy the layers.
5. Roll out into a 40x70 cm rectangle. Dust the work surface with flour during the process. Lift the dough every now and then to prevent it from contracting. Be careful not to ruin the shape of the rectangle. The ideal thickness is 2.5 mm.
6. Trim the edges with a sharp knife and divide the rectangle in two using a sharp knife, use a ruler.
7. Trace eight triangles with a 12 cm base, then cut with a sharp knife. Arrange on a surface lightly dusted with flour and cover with cling-film. Leave to set for 30 minutes.
8. Place the triangles, one at a time, on the work surface with the apex towards you. Pull at the two corners at the base and roll into a crescent starting at the base. Roll with one hand while holding the apex with the other. Make sure the apex ends up in the middle underneath the roll to prevent it from rising in the oven.
9. Place on two baking trays, 9 on each, and bend into a crescent-shape. Since the walls are the hottest parts of the oven, the ends should be turned towards the centre of the tray. Glaze with beaten egg with a pinch of salt. Brush from the centre towards the edge to prevent the layers from sticking together.

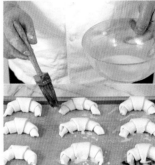

10. Leave to rise for 90–120 minutes until doubled in size in a cold oven, max. 30°C, or the butter will melt. The ideal temperature is 24°. Remove.
11. Preheat the oven to 230°C . Glaze the croissants again, gently, using a brush. Bake for 15 minutes until golden brown.
12. Take out the croissants and leave to cool on a wire rack.

Petits pains au chocolat

16 petits pains

1 batch Croissant dough, see p. 191

200 g dark chocolate   egg for glazing
  (e.g. Valrhona Grand Cru
  Guanaja 70%)

1. Cut the rolled out dough into two strips and divide each into eight equally-sized pieces.
2. Divide 200 g dark chocolate (room temperature) into 16 equally-sized pieces.
3. Whisk the egg and glaze the squares. Place a piece of chocolate on each. Fold into three, see picture below, and place eight on each tray seam down.
4. Glaze with egg and leave to rise as for Croissants.
5. Bake at 190–200°C for 12–15 minutes.
6. Immediately transfer to cool on a wire rack.

Freeze in plastic bags as soon as they are cold, heat in 200°C and they will be as good as fresh.

Useful information
There are two types of rolled-out, layered doughs: with or without yeast. How does the rising process work?
Yeast doughs rise because of the carbon dioxide that is formed during rising and from the steam pressure that is created during baking. The dough is folded three times for croissants, Danish pastries and Tebirkes, i.e. 27 layers of butter and 28 layers of dough. The basic rolled-out dough should not develop the gluten fully since the dough is stretched during rolling. If it gets too elastic, the butter layers will break, and the dough will be ruined.

Danish Pastries

Legend has it that itinerant apprentices from Austria were the first to make these in Denmark. In German-speaking countries Danish pastries are called Plundergebäck.

I can still remember how good the Danish pastries with freshly made apple jam flavoured with cinnamon and vanilla custard tasted. The classic, square Danish pastries are called Spandauer.

approx. 30 Danish pastries

VANILLA CUSTARD
1/2 vanilla pod, preferably from Tahiti
500 g full-fat milk (5 dl)
120 g egg (appr. 6)
125 g sugar
40 g corn starch
25 g butter

PASTRY DOUGH
600 g strong wheat flour
250 g water (2.5 dl)

50 g yeast
100 g egg (appr. 2)
40 g egg yolk (appr. 2)
35 g sugar
10 g sea salt
625 g unsalted butter

1 egg with a pinch of salt for glazing

almond flakes

VANILLA CUSTARD
1. Split the vanilla pod lengthwise, scrape out the seeds into a small saucepan and add the milk.
2. Bring to the boil, set aside, put the lid on and leave the milk to absorb the vanilla flavour.
3. Whisk egg yolks and sugar until fluffy and add the flour. Pour over the milk and mix carefully. Pour back in the saucepan.
4. Bring to the boil while stirring.
5. Add the butter and whisk until it has melted. Pour it through a sieve into a flat tin. Cover with cling-film and cool in cold water. Keep in the fridge until needed. It will keep for two days at the most.

PASTRY DOUGH
1. Prepare the dough by cooling the flour in the fridge for 1 hour before making the dough.
2. Pour the water into a 2 l bowl and dissolve the yeast using a whisk. Add egg, egg yolk, sugar and salt and work by hand until the dough no longer sticks to the edge of the bowl, or work in a mixer for 2–3 minutes.
3. Wrap in cling film and freeze for 15 minutes.

4. Turn out on a floured work surface and roll out to a 35x20 cm square. Soften the cold butter by beating it with the rolling pin while it is still cold.

5. Fold the corners over the butter so that it is completely covered. Wrap in cling-film and leave in the fridge for 30 minutes so that the dough and butter will have the same temperature.

6. Lightly dust the work surface with flour and gently roll out the dough into a 45x75 cm rectangle starting at the centre. Fold the ends to make three layers (see p. 192).

7. Turn the rectangle 90° on the floured surface. Gently roll out again as above. Fold in three.

8. Wrap in cling-film and leave to set for 30 minutes in the fridge. Roll out again and fold. The dough is now ready to use.

9. Roll out the dough approx. 4 mm thick. Sprinkle a small amount of flour on top and underneath the dough. Trim the edges with a knife and cut out square pieces using a ruler, 9x9 cm.

10. Fill a plastic bag with *remonce* (see below). Cut a hole and squeeze out a round ball, approx. 10 g, in the middle of the pastry.

11. Fold the corners to make an "envelope" and firmly press with your thumb in the middle so the pastries do not come undone during proving. Place on a baking tray covered with a greased baking sheet and leave to rise under a tea-towel for 45–60 minutes or until doubled in size.

12. Whisk an egg with a pinch of salt and glaze the pastries gently. Press with your thumb in the centre. Pour the cold custard into an icing bag, cut a hole and squeeze out 20 g of custard on each pastry. Sprinkle with almond slivers.

13. Preheat the oven to 220°C.

14. Bake for 14–15 minutes until golden brown. Remove the tray and cool on a wire rack.

Most bakers glaze their Danish pastries with a white fondant or water glaze, which I find too sweet.

REMONCE
100 g almonds
100 g sugar
50 g butter
25 g plain flour

1. Bring the water to the boil in a saucepan, add the almonds and scald. Pour the almonds into a sieve and rinse with cold water. Turn out on the work surface and remove the skins.

2. Mix almonds and sugar until smooth. Add butter and plain flour and mix into a thick batter.

Tebirkes

These delicious breakfast rolls are often served in Danish cafés. (Picture p. 193)

approx. 30 rolls

950 g strong wheat flour, preferably stone ground	500 g unsalted butter for rolling
50 g yeast	1 egg and a pinch of salt for glazing
500 g full-fat milk (5 dl)	100 g each black and white poppy seeds
50 g butter	
15 g honey	
50 g egg (1)	
15 g sea salt	

1. Pour the wheat flour onto a sheet of paper and place in the fridge for 60 minutes before making the dough.
2. Dissolve the yeast in the cold milk with a whisk. Melt butter and honey.
3. Weigh flour, egg and salt and pour over the milk. Knead the dough. Add butter and honey and knead on the lowest speed for approx. 5 minutes until almost elastic.
4. Flatten the dough on a plastic bag dusted with flour and leave to set for 30 minutes in the fridge.
5. Place on a work top dusted with flour and roll into a 35x20 cm rectangle. Soften the butter by beating it with the rolling pin several times to soften it while still cold.
6. Fold the corners and cover the butter completely. Wrap the dough in cling-film. Leave for 30 minutes in the fridge so that the butter and the dough acquire the same temperature.
7. Lightly flour the work surface and gently roll out the dough, working from the centre towards the edges, until you have a 45x75 cm triangle. Fold to make three layers (see p. 192).
8. Turn the rectangle 90° on the lightly floured work surface. Gently roll out again from the centre towards the edges as above. Fold into three.
9. Wrap in cling-film and leave to set for 30 minutes in the fridge.
10. Roll out again as before. The dough is now ready to use.
11. Roll out a 3 mm thick strips and cut into 200 mm wide sections. Glaze on one side with egg and a pinch of salt.
12. Fold into three and flip over seam down. Glaze with egg and sprinkle generously with poppy seeds. Cut off 50 g pieces.
13. Place on a baking tray covered with paper and cover with a tea-towel. Leave to rise at room temperature for 60–75 minutes until doubled in size.
14. Preheat the oven to 220°C and bake for 15 minutes until golden brown. Cool on a wire rack.

Serve fresh with breakfast.

"Remember that flour is a perishable product and that it does not improve by storing."

Jam

Below are three of my favourite jams and a great jelly. The jelly is very tart since it contains no sugar.

Strawberry and Rhubarb Jam

1,000 g rhubarb, peeled and rinsed	1,600 g sugar
1,000 g strawberries, ripe, topped and rinsed	150 g lemon juice (1.5 dl)
	12 g citric acid (12 ml)

DAY 1

Dice the rhubarb. Mix with the hulled strawberries, sugar and lemon juice. Cover with cling-film and marinate over night, 24 hours.

DAY 2

1. Drain the fruit in a sieve for 60 minutes. Pour the juice in a 10 l cooking pot and boil until 110°C.
2. Add the drained fruit to the pot and boil until 107°C. Remove from the heat and stir in the citric acid, thus activating the pectin in the berries.
3. Clean the jars and heat to 80°C. Fill immediately with the hot jam up to the rim, tighten the lids and turn the jars upside down.

Apricot and Almond Jam

400 g almonds, preferably Spanish or Italian	2 vanilla pods, preferably from Tahiti
2,000 g scalded apricots, stones removed (approx. 2,500 g fresh)	1,600 g sugar
	150 g lemon juice
	10 g citric acid (2 tsp)

Bring 1 l of water to the boil, scald the almonds and rinse in cold water. Peel and set aside.

Scald the apricots in boiling water and transfer them to cold water. Split the vanilla pod lengthwise and mix with the sugar, apricots, almonds and lemon juice in a large 10 l flat-bottomed cooking pot.

Continue as for Strawberry and Rhubarb Jam.

Fig Jam with Fresh Bay Leaves and Black Pepper

Serve with a slice of toasted brioche or a slice of goose or duck liver with a little flaky salt and pepper. (Remember that goose and duck liver should not be served cold, it will spoil the whole experience.)

2,000 g fresh, rinsed, figs, stems removed	20 fresh bay leaves
1,600 g sugar	10 crushed black pepper corns
250 g lemon juice	12 g citric acid (12 ml)

Clean the figs, remove the stalks and quarter. Mix with sugar, lemon juice, bay leaves and crushed black pepper corns in a 10 l pot.

Boil as for Strawberry and Rhubarb Jam

Blackberry Jelly

This jelly goes wonderfully well with brioches, croissants or weggelis, or Sunday roast.

2,000 ripe blackberries
500 g water (5 dl)

Approx. 650 g sugar

1. Clean and rinse the berries, drain. Boil in the water on low heat with a lid for 15 minutes.
2. Pour into a damp cheesecloth and drain for 60 minutes.
3. Measure the juice, it should be approx. 650 g.
4. Bring the juice to the boil and skim. Remove from the heat and stir in an equal amount of sugar to the amount of juice, i.e. 650 g. Stir until it has melted. Pour into jars that have been heated to 80°C. Fill up to the rim, screw the lid on tight immediately and turn the jars upside down.

SWEET DOUGHS

Kugelhopf

Kougloufs, or kouglofs, there are many names and spellings for this Alsatian specialty. In Switzerland it is called kugelhopf, and I remember from my Swiss days that these were very popular at the weekend. We used to make a stirred variety covered with chocolate icing, which was called choc-kugelhopf. Along the Route des Vins in Alsace they make them in special clay moulds that you can buy to take home as a souvenir.

Serve fresh with a glass of good wine and a slice of goose liver terrine, or a cup of coffee. (Picture p. 196).

2 cake tins as shown on p. 196, 1.5 l
Ideal dough temperature 28°C

200 g raisins	25 g yeast
50 g dark rum or	100 g full-fat milk (1 dl)
Kirschwasser (0.5 dl)	350 g butter
500 g strong wheat flour,	200 g almonds
preferably stone ground	
15 g sea salt	25 g butter and
70 g sugar	10 g wheat flour for the
300 g egg (approx. 6)	moulds

DAY 1

1. Soak the raisins in the rum. Cover with cling-film and leave for 24 hours.
2. Weigh wheat flour, salt and sugar in a bowl and pour over the eggs.
3. Dissolve the yeast in the milk and pour into the bowl. Knead on the lowest speed for 15 minutes.
4. Add butter a little at a time and increase the speed now and then until all the butter has been absorbed. Knead for approx. 20 minutes until very elastic.
5. Place the dough in a plastic container with a lid and leave to rise for 2 hours at room temperature.
6. Turn out on a work surface, knock back and fold into a pillow-shape. Replace in the container and leave in the fridge until the next day min. 18 and max. 24 hours.

DAY 2

1. Bring a little water to the boil and scald the almonds for 1 minute. Place in a colander, rinse under cold water and remove the skins.
2. Grease two moulds with the soft butter, dust with wheat flour and shake out the surplus.
3. Place whole almonds at the bottom of the mould.
4. Cut the remaining almonds into slivers.
5. Place the dough on a floured work surface, sprinkle with raisins and almonds and mix.
6. Divide the dough in two and make two balls, cover with a tea-towel and leave for 10 minutes.
7. Thread the balls over the centre of the mould.
8. Cover and leave to rise until the moulds are 3/4 filled, Approx. 150 minutes depending on the room temperature.
9. Preheat the oven to 220°C. When it is warm, place the moulds in the oven.
10. Lower the temperature to 200°C after 5 minutes. Open the oven door after another 10 minutes to let some air in.
11. Bake for approx. 45 minutes. Use a thermometer to check if the breads are ready (98°C).
12. Take the breads out of the oven, turn out on the tray, put them back and bake for another 5 minutes. Place on a wire rack to cool.
13. Sift icing sugar over the finished breads.

Freeze in plastic bags and warm up gently, inside the bag, and it will be as good as fresh.

Tip
This bread is very good to toast. Dip leftover slices in pancake batter, fry in butter, turn over in cinnamon and sugar. This is very nice with whipped cream and lingonberry jam.

VARIATION

During a wine trip in the Alsace I visited a patisserie in Münster, famous for its cheese, where I was offered another variation: instead of raisins there were 100 g smoked ham, 25 g chopped parsley, 25 g finely cut chives and 50 g grated strong cheese seasoned with nutmeg. It was amazingly good.

Pain d'épices

This spicy French bread, something between cake and bread, is very nice with cheese. This is typical of the Alsace region. (Picture p. 202)

I got this recipe from the world champion of bread making, Émile Cauvière, when I attended a course at the École Nationale Supérieure de la Pâtisserie-Glacerie-Chocolaterie. Always use freshly ground spices.

2 rectangular 2 l sponge cake tins.

DAY 1	DAY 2
15 g star anise, finely ground in an electric mill	375 g strong wheat flour
20 g cinnamon from Sri Lanka, finely ground	125 g fine rye flour or chestnut flour
475 g set honey	25 g bicarbonate of soda
425 g full-fat milk (4.25 dl)	125 g candied orange peel, finely chopped
125 g light muscovado or cassonade sugar	1 ripe lemon
	25 g butter for the tin
	60 g flaked almonds for the tin

DAY 1
1. Grind the spices in an electric mill.
2. Weigh the honey, milk and sugar in a 2 l stainless steel saucepan.
3. Add the spices and bring to the boil while stirring.
4. Remove from the heat and pour into a 4 l metal bowl. Cover with cling film.

DAY 2
1. Sift the flours and the bicarbonate of soda on to a paper. Finely chop the candied orange peel. Wash and dry the lemon and grate only the yellow part.
2. Mix the flour mixture into the honey batter with a wooden spoon until smooth. Add orange peel and grated lemon and mix carefully.
3. Preheat the oven to 150°C.
4. Use a soft brush to grease the tins with the soft butter. Sprinkle the flaked almonds around the inside of the tin.
5. Fill about half the tin with batter.
6. Bake for 60–80 minutes. Check that the centre of the cake is dry.
7. Remove the cakes from the oven and leave in the tin to the side of the stove for 5 minutes.
8. Turn out on a wire rack and cool.

The Pain d'épices keeps for about a week in an airtight bag or container. In the freezer it keeps for months if well wrapped in plastic.

Tip
A recipe for candied orange peel can be found in my book Chocolate.

Tea Cakes

This Swedish classic is ideal as a sandwich base. (Picture pp. 56 and 200)

One of my former students, Carina Håkansson, loves these more than anything. In her honour, I created extra soft teacakes. Carina would happily munch on these during her lunch break at the test bakery.

This recipe is also suitable for making layered sandwich cakes.

Approx. 30 teacakes, 60 g each
Ideal dough temperature 28°C.

50 g yeast	150 g butter
500 g full-fat milk (5 dl)	25 g sugar
15 g honey	15 g salt
950 g strong wheat flour	

STARTER
Dissolve the yeast in the milk, add honey and half of the flour. Whisk until fluffy. Cover and leave to rise in a warm place for 30 minutes.

KNEADING
1. Place the remaining ingredients, except the salt, into the bowl and pour over the risen dough. Knead for 10 minutes on low speed, then add the salt. Knead for another 10 minutes until very elastic. Increase the speed somewhat towards the end for even greater elasticity.

Continued on p. 200

2. Place in a lightly oiled plastic container with a lid. Leave for 60 minutes. Knock back after 30 minutes.

3. Turn out on a floured work surface and divide in two.

4. Roll out and cut off 60 g pieces, use scales. Make balls, cover and leave for 5 minutes. Roll out round, flat cakes with the help of a little wheat flour and prick with a fork.

5. Place 12 cakes on each tray covered in paper, cover and leave for 45 minutes until doubled in size.

6. Preheat the oven to 250°. Spray with water to dampen the air.

7. Put the tray in the oven and bake for 8 minutes until the cakes are golden brown.

8. Take out the tray and leave to cool on a wire rack.

VARIATIONS

• Replace 300 g of the wheat flour with coarse wholemeal flour and the sugar with brown muscovado sugar for a more rustic bread.

• Replace 250 g of the wheat flour with 250 g coarse rye flour and add 10 g whole caraway seeds. Mix in 150 g lightly roasted sunflower seeds at the end.

Suitable for freezing in plastic bags.

Teacakes

Soft Gingerbread from Skåne

This specialty is as important to a Swede from Skåne as the regional dark rye and scalded sweet and sour breads. I remember having these gingerbreads with butter and strong cheese for tea at my grandmother's house.

Approx. 30 ginger breads

DAY 1	
1,250 g plain flour	12.5 g potash
10 g freshly ground cloves	50 g water (0.5 dl)
8 g freshly ground dried ginger	12.5 bicarbonate of soda
9 dl golden syrup	50 g water (0.5 dl)
	15 g ammonium carbonate
	50 g water (0.5 dl)

DAY 1

1. Mix wheat flour and freshly ground spices. Use an electric mill if you have one.

2. Add syrup and mix.

3. Dissolve the potash, bicarbonate of soda and ammonium carbonate in their respective amounts of water, pour into the bowl. Knead into a dough.

4. Place in a lightly oiled plastic container with a lid. Leave in the fridge for at least 24 hours.

DAY 2

1. Turn out the dough and knead by hand. Roll out until 1 cm thick and cut out cakes the size of a saucer. Put on a tray covered with a baking sheet. Brush with milk to make them glossy.

2. Preheat the oven to 180°C and bake for 14–15 minutes until golden brown. Remove the tray and leave to cool on a wire rack. Keep in a jar or in the freezer.

Potassium carbonate, or potash, is used for some gingerbread doughs, especially in Germany and Switzerland. It is hygroscopic and used to keep the cakes soft. Bicarbonate of soda and ammonium carbonate act as rising agents as they react with the gluten in the flour.

Soft Gingerbread from Skåne.

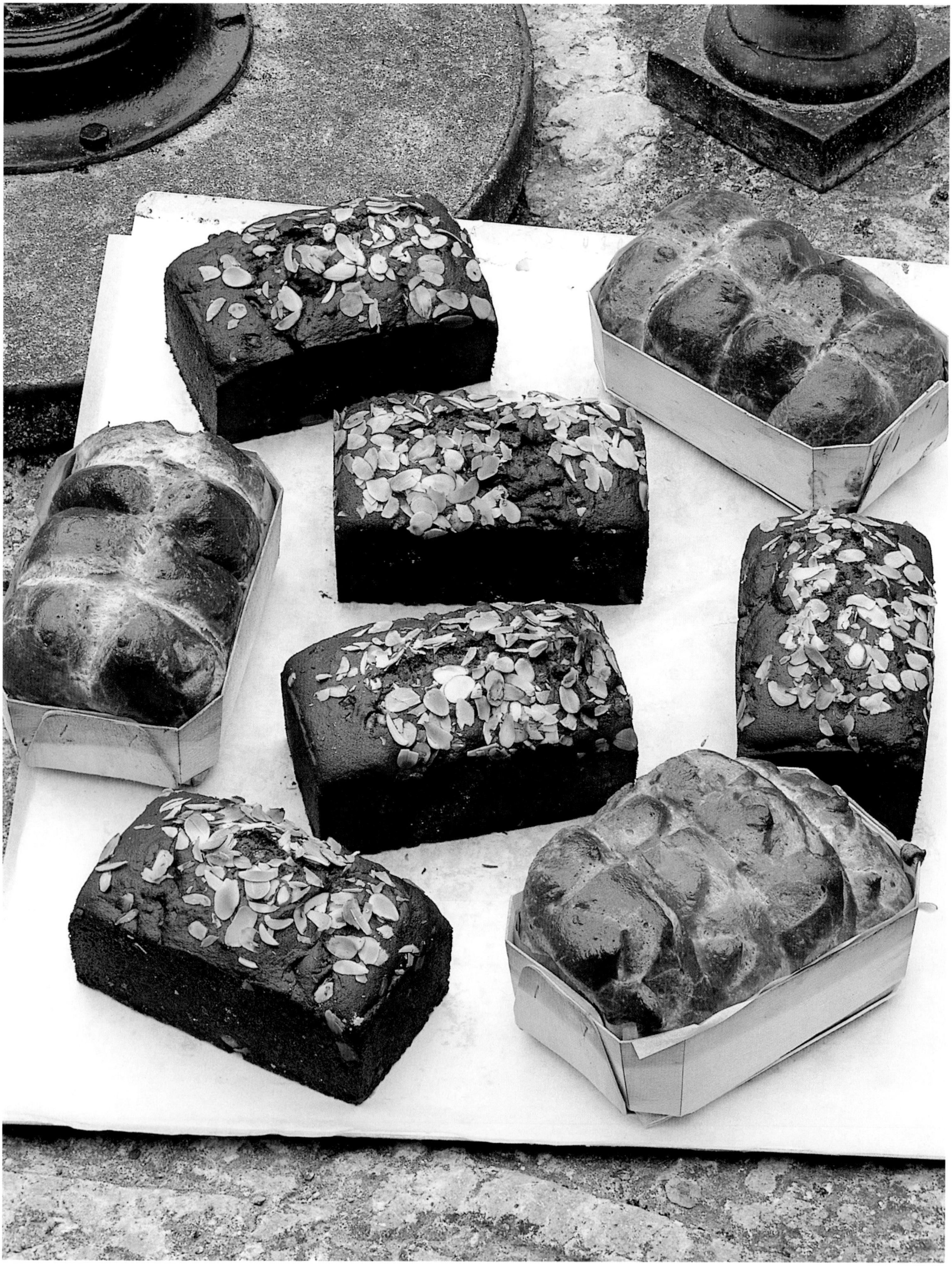

Pain d'épices (p. 199) and Brioche Nanterre (p. 188).

Flat Rye Cakes (p. 204) and rusks (p. 205).

Rolf's Bread

Rolf Augustsson used to run a patisserie in Malmö for many years, and we worked together during one period. Rolf came from the province of Småland and loved sweet bread. These bread cakes were always to be found in his window display.

4 breads
Ideal dough temperature 26°.

300 g coarse rye flour	15 g whole fennel seed
600 g strong wheat flour, preferably stone ground	30 g yeast
	500 g water (5 dl)
150 g golden syrup	20 g salt
15 g whole aniseed	50 g butter

1. Weigh the flour, syrup and spices in the bowl.
2. Dissolve the yeast in the water and pour over the other ingredients except salt and butter. Knead the dough on low speed for 10 minutes.
3. Add salt and butter and knead for approx. 5 minutes until elastic.
4. Place in a lightly oiled plastic container with a lid and leave for 60 minutes, knock back once during rising.
5. Turn out on a floured work surface and divide into four pieces. Make round balls, cover with a tea-towel and leave for 5 minutes.
6. Roll out round cakes the size of a dinner plate using rye flour and prick with a fork.
7. Use a small cutter to cut a whole in the centre.
8. Place on two trays, cover with a tea-towel and leave to rise until doubled in size for 60 minutes.

9. Preheat the oven to 250° and bake one tray at a time when the oven is hot. Spray with water.
10. Bake for approx. 15 minutes until golden brown.
11. Cool on a wire rack.

Suitable for freezing in plastic bags.

Flat Rye Cakes

This soft bread from the province of Bohuslän on the west coast of Sweden is used for sandwiches. (Picture p. 203)

6 cakes
Ideal dough temperature 26°C.

50 g yeast	2 g ground fennel seeds
500 g full-fat milk (5 dl)	2 g ground aniseed
500 g strong wheat flour, preferably stone ground	75 g sugar
	100 g butter
500 g rye flour/wheat flour blend	15 g sea salt

1. Dissolve the yeast in the milk, on low speed, and add flour, spices and sugar.
2. Knead on low speed for 2 minutes. Add the soft butter and kneed on low speed for 8 minutes. Add the salt and knead for 8 minutes until elastic.
3. Place the dough in a lightly oiled lidded plastic container and leave for 60 minutes. Knock back after half the time.
4. Turn out on a floured work surface and divide into 6 250 g pieces. Make round balls, cover with a tea-towel and leave for 10 minutes.
5. Roll out round, flat cakes, with a diameter of 250 mm and 3 mm thick using wheat flour.
6. Place on a baking tray and prick deep with a fork. Cover with a tea-towel and leave to rise until doubled in size for approx. 60 minutes.
7. Preheat the oven to 250°C.
8. Bake for 8–10 minutes until light brown.
9. Transfer to a tea-towel, cover with another towel to keep the bread soft.

Suitable for freezing in plastic bags.

Basic Sweet Dough

I use a starter to make a basic sweet white dough since it improves rising properties. Use this basic recipe for all traditional sweet wheat doughs.

STARTER	KNEADING
700 g strong wheat flour	175 g sugar
25 g sugar	10 g salt
75 g yeast	50 g egg (1)
500 g full-fat milk (5 dl)	20 g cardamom, ground with pestle and mortar
	500 g strong wheat flour, preferably stone ground
	250 g butter

Make as for Christmas Bread, p. 211.

If you want to make plain buns, follow the instructions for Wheat Rusks up until point 7.

Karlsbad Buns

When I started out in the business, most bakers made wheat dough, pastry dough, and sometimes Danish pastry dough with a little wheat flour and a few eggs. This light and fluffy dough is called "Karlsbad" dough.

This is my version, which is extremely light and fluffy. Use it for all kinds of traditional sweet doughs.

STARTER	KNEADING
375 g strong wheat flour, preferably stone ground	55 g sugar
25 g sugar	10 g salt
50 g yeast	80 g egg (4)
250 g full-fat milk (2.5 dl)	500 g strong wheat flour
	125 g butter
	200 g full-fat milk (2 dl)

Make as for Christmas Bread, p. 211.

If you want to make plain buns, follow the instructions for Wheat Rusks up until point 7.

Wheat Rusks

This dough is ideal for flaky, delicious rusks. Always keep in an air-tight tin.

approx. 50 buns or 100 rusks

1 batch basic sweet dough

1 egg and a pinch of salt for glazing

See recipe for Christmas Bread, p. 211 and follow the instructions up to point 3 under Kneading.

1. Place the dough on a floured work surface and divide into 400 g pieces. Roll into long strips and cut each into ten pieces.
2. Make oblong "hot dog rolls" and place 12 on each baking tray. For buns, make round buns instead.
3. Cover with a tea-towel and leave to rise until doubled in size for approx. 60 minutes.
4. Whisk an egg with a pinch of salt and glace.
5. Preheat the oven to 230°C.
6. Bake for 12 minutes until golden brown.
7. Cool on a wire rack.
8. Split open with a fork and return the halves to the tray.
9. Lower the temperature to 150°C . Bake until golden brown and turn off the oven. Open the oven door so the rusks can dry until brittle.

Wholemeal rusks
Replace 550 g of the wheat flour in the wheat dough with wholemeal flour and proceed as for wheat rusks.

Karlsbad rusks
Make a "Karlsbad" dough and make buns as for wheat rusks.

Rye rusks
Replace 350 g of the wheat flour in the wheat dough with coarse rye flour and make as for wheat rusks.

Dresdner Weihnachtsstollen

CHRISTMAS

Wort Bread

Most Swedes cannot imagine Christmas without wort bread. When I was 16, working at a patisserie in Malmö, the brewer's truck used to deliver the wort. My job was to boil it until half the amount remained and then pour it into milk churns.

This is a moist, tasty bread that keeps for several days. The three stages of baking are typical of breads from the province of Skåne. (Picture p. 206 and opposite)

4 loaves
Ideal dough temperature 28°C.

SCALDING 1	
200 g small beer (2 dl)	6 g ground Seville orange peel
100 g fine rye flour	2 g ground cloves
	4 g ground ginger
SCALDING 2	3 g ground cardamom
100 g small beer (1 dl)	100 g fine rye flour, preferably stone ground
80 g yeast	
100 g fine rye flour	1,000 g strong wheat flour, preferably stone ground
KNEADING	40 g butter
140 g small beer (1.4 dl)	20 g salt
260 g dark syrup	
200 g liquid brewer's wort (2 dl)	160 g raisins
	25 g butter for glazing

SCALDING 1
Bring the small beer to the boil and immediately pour it over the flour in the bowl. Stir until smooth using a dough hook for approx. 30 minutes. Make sure that the temperature is reduced to 50°C.

SCALDING 2
Add the small beer and mix well. Add yeast and rye flour and knead for 10 minutes. Cover with a tea-towel and leave to rise for 30 minutes. Soak the raisins in plenty of cold water and leave for 30 minutes. Drain in a sieve.

KNEADING
1. Heat the small beer, syrup, wort and spices to 35°C. Pour over the second scalding and add flour, butter and salt. Knead on low speed for 12 minutes. Increase the speed and work until very elastic for another 5 minutes.
2. Sprinkle a pinch of wheat flour over the raisins before mixing them into the dough to make them blend more easily.
3. Place the dough in a lightly oiled plastic container with a lid and leave for 45 minutes. Knock back after half the time.
4. Turn out on a floured work surface and divide into four. Make balls, cover with a towel and leave for 10 minutes. Shape four oblong loaves. Place two on each tray, spray with water and place in the unheated oven. Leave to rise until doubled in size, approx. 60 minutes. Spray with water twice during rising to prevent a crust from forming and the bread cracking up during baking. Remove the breads from the oven.
5. Preheat the oven with the stone or tray to 250°C.
6. Place one of the trays in a cool place to prevent rising.
7. Move the loaves to the stone or hot tray with a spatula and spray a little water into the oven.
8. Lower the temperature to 200°C after 5 minutes. Open the oven door after another 10 minutes to let some air in. Repeat twice during baking.
9. Bake for 45 minutes. Use a thermometer to check that the bread is ready (98°C).
10. Remove from the oven and glaze with melted butter. Cool on a wire rack. Repeat with the other two loaves.

Tips
Make well before Christmas and freeze in plastic bags. If you cannot get hold of brewer's wort you can boil down 1,000 g small beer to 200 g and use that instead.

Wort Bread.

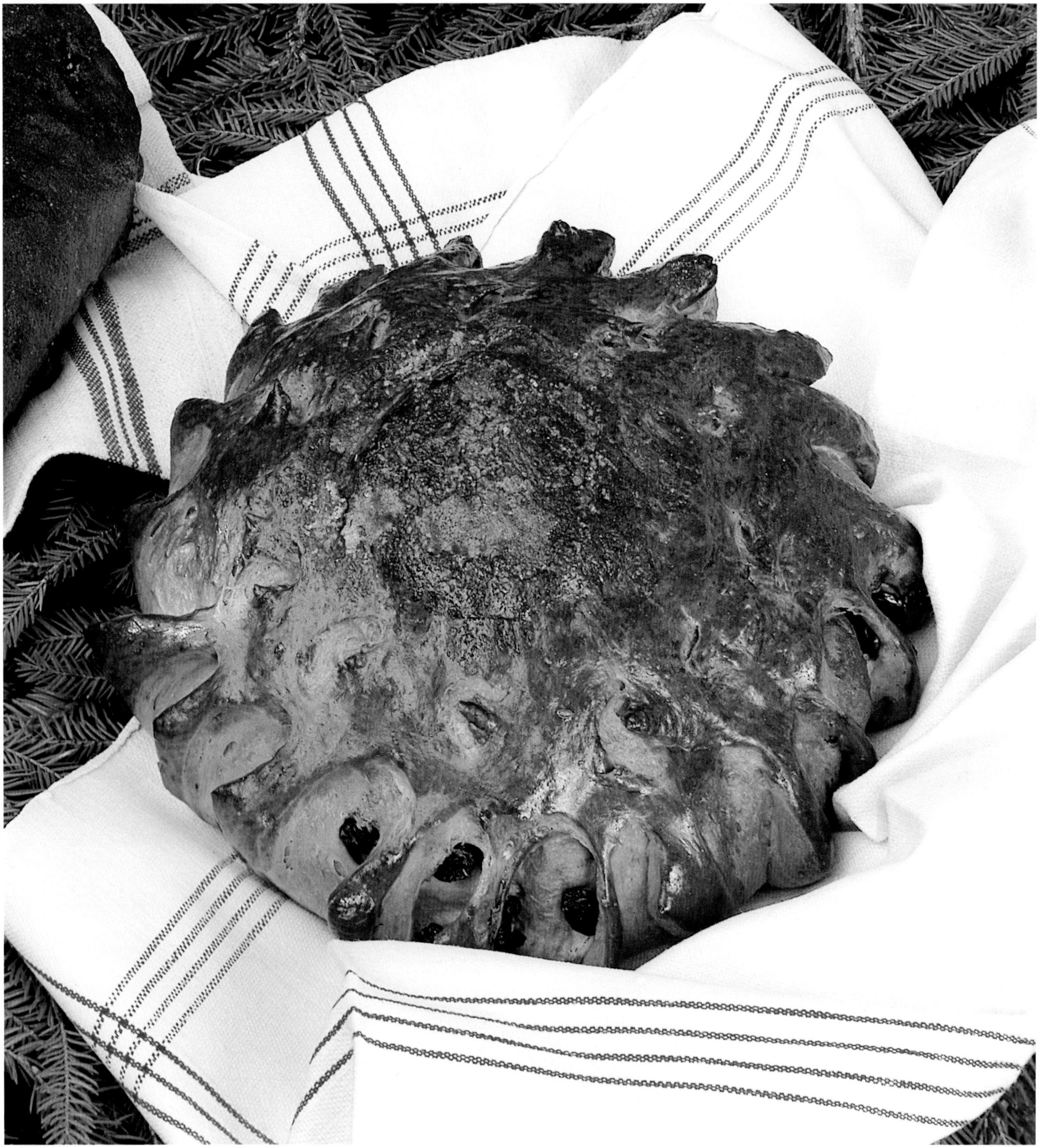

Christmas Loaf.

Sweet Christmas Loaf

There would be no Christmas without a sweet loaf flavoured with saffron and cardamom. This only exists in Sweden, Norway and Finland, the only countries in the world that use saffron and cardamom to flavour sweet bread.

To make it extra moist, I make a special dough, with extra sugar and butter as well as an egg, which is not normally included in this type of dough. I usually add the egg because it makes the loaf lighter and better tasting. For an attractive, glossy loaf, glaze twice with egg yolk and water.

I prefer the light-green cardamom from Sri Lanka for sweet dough. Cardamom is often bleached, whereby it loses much of its aroma. Toast the cardamom until the shells come off and remove. Crush coarsely in a pestle and mortar. The flavour is infinitely superior to the shop bought version.

2 Christmas breads
Ideal dough temperature 26°C.

STARTER	
400 g strong wheat flour, preferably stone ground	450 g strong wheat flour
25 g sugar	200 g butter
50 g yeast	
250 g full-fat milk (2.5 dl)	50 g chopped almond, skins removed
	100 g raisins
KNEADING	100 g diced candied peel
100 g sugar	
10 g sea salt	2 egg yolks and a pinch of salt for glazing
50 g egg	50 g chopped almonds, skins removed, for decoration
15 g cardamom, crushed	
3 g powdered saffron	

1. Briefly whisk 2 egg yolks, 1 tbsp water and a pinch of salt. Use for glazing.
2. Scald 100 g almonds in boiling water and rinse with cold water. Remove the skins, chop coarsely and leave to dry on kitchen paper.
3. Soak the raisins in plenty of cold water for 30 minutes and drain in a sieve.
4. If possible, use whole candied peel and dice it.

STARTER

Weigh the flour and sugar in a bowl. Dissolve the yeast in the milk and pour over the flour. Work on low speed for 10 minutes. Place the dough in a lightly oiled plastic container with a lid and leave to rise in a warm place for 30–45 minutes until doubled in size.

KNEADING

1. Weigh the sugar and salt and pour on top of the starter. Add eggs, spices and flour and knead on low speed for 5–6 minutes. Add the butter in small chunks, increase the speed and knead for another 10 minutes until very elastic. Test the dough for elasticity.
2. If you are making Christmas Loaf, mix in the fruit and almonds.
3. Place the dough in a lightly oiled plastic container with a lid and leave to rise for 30 minutes.
4. Divide in two and shape tight balls. Cover with a towel and leave for 5 minutes.
5. Place the balls on two trays covered with baking paper and press them flat with your hand. Use a pair of scissors to cut a pattern around the edge, see opposite page. Glaze with egg yolk and sprinkle with almonds. Put both trays in an unheated oven and leave to rise for 34–60 minutes until doubled in size.
6. Take out the trays and preheat the oven to 220°C. Glaze again with egg yolk and sprinkle with castor sugar.
7. Put one tray in the oven and the other in a cool place to prevent it from rising too much.
8. Lower the temperature to 190°C after 5 minutes. If the temperature is too high, the breads will collapse in the middle when removed from the oven. Bake for 25–30 minutes until golden brown.
9. Take out the bread and leave to cool on a wire rack. Repeat with the other tray.

Panettone

This is a legendary Italian bread that is made all over the world for Christmas. It is usually made with ordinary yeast, and therefore it dries out quickly. At the prestigious patisseries of Milan, you can try a version made with apple yeast.

Panettone is one of the most complicated sweet doughs you there is, so you might as well make four while you are at it, they keep for a long time. Delicious with a cup of coffee or a glass of wine.

4 panettone
Ideal dough temperature 28ºC.
4 round high-edged tins, 22 cm diameter.

STARTER	
100 g sugar	grated rind of 1/2 a washed orange
160 g water (1.6 dl)	1 vanilla pod, preferably from Tahiti
400 g strong wheat flour	
200 g "chef", p. 31	50 g sugar
10 g honey	120 g softned butter
100 g soft butter	30 g water (0.3 dl)
120 g egg yolk (6 eggs)	150 g California raisins
	50 g candied orange peel, diced finely
KNEADING	50 g candied lemon peel
150 g strong wheat flour, preferably stone ground	
10 g sea salt grated rind of 1/2 a washed lemon	25 g butter for greasing

STARTER

1. Mix sugar and water to make a syrup. The water temperature should be 22ºC. Add flour and "chef" in a bowl together with the syrup and honey. Knead on the lowest speed for 15 minutes.
2. Mix in the soft butter and egg yolks. Knead on slightly higher speed until elastic. If it starts to get shiny, it has been kneaded for too long.
3. Place the dough in a lightly oiled plastic container with a lid and leave at a temperature of 24–26ºC. Leave to rise for 10–12 hours or until tripled in size. If it does not rise properly now, the next step will take longer.

KNEADING

1. Pour the risen starter into a bowl.
2. Add wheat flour, salt, lemon and orange rind and the seeds scraped from the vanilla pod.
3. Add sugar, half of the egg yolks and keep kneading for 2 minutes. Add 20 g of the butter, which must be soft, and the rest of the egg yolks. Increase the speed and knead for 3 minutes until very elastic. Test the dough for elasticity. Add water and mix it in.
4. Melt 20 g butter and mix into the dough together with the fruit. Knead for 3–4 minutes until the fruit is well mixed in.
5. Turn out on a floured work surface and check the texture. It should bounce back under pressure. If it does not, it is not elastic enough.
6. Divide in two and make four tight balls. Place on a tea-towel dusted with flour on a baking tray and cover. Place in the oven (28ºC) or in a warm place and leave to rise for 40 minutes. Take out the balls and knock back. Make 4 new tight balls and put these in four circular, greased tins.
7. Place in the turned-off oven or at 30–32ºC, which is the ideal temperature.
8. Leave until the dough starts to rise over the top. Spray with water a couple of times so it does not dry out. This may take 6–7 hours depending on the elasticity.
9. Cut a cross on top of the breads and put dollops of butter inside (40 g). Place in the oven.
10. Preheat the oven to 180°C and remove the breads after 5 minutes. Lift up the four points to make them fold. Return to the oven and bake for 45–50 minutes, use a thermometer to check that the temperature at the centre is 98°.

The Panettone increases by several times its original size in the oven. How much it rises depends on the amount of fruit that has been added.

Turn out directly after baking for the breads to keep their shape. Leave for 10–12 hours before packing in plastic bags.

Dresdner Weihnachtsstollen (p. 214), Decorative Bread (p. 218) and Panettone (p. 212).

Yule Log

Christmas is not the same without a real stollen, or Yule log. (Picture p. 207 and 213).

I remember from Switzerland how we turned out these breads all day every day in December. We were out in the yard, dipping them twice in melted butter before turning them over in sugar. Stollen is a German Christmas tradition famous all over the world.

This is a marvellous recipe provided you follow it to the letter.

2 stollen
Ideal dough temperature 28°C.

DAY 1

ALMOND PASTE
150 g almonds
150 g sugar

SOAKING
50 g slivered almonds
50 g candied orange peel, chopped
50 g mixed candied peel, chopped
240 g California raisins
0.5 dl dark rum

DAY 2

STARTER
250 g strong wheat flour
15 g sugar
50 g yeast
165 g fulll-fat milk (1.65 dl)

KNEADING
1 vanilla pod
2 g ground cardamom
1 g ground nutmeg
2 g ground tonka beans
20 g almonds, skins removed
15 g bitter almonds
grated rind of 1 washed lemon
20 g sugar
250 g strong wheat flour
1 egg yolk
75 g sugar
5 g salt
125 g butter

VANILLA SUGAR
1 vanilla pod, cut up
50 g icing sugar
25 g potato flour

Mix the vanilla pod with sugar and potato flour. Sift.

DAY 1

ALMOND PASTE
Scald the almonds in boiling water, place in a colander and rinse under cold running water. Remove the skins and place in a mixer together with the sugar. Mix until smooth, then put the resulting paste in a plastic bag. Leave overnight.

SOAKING
Scald the almonds in boiling water, place in a colander and rinse under cold running water. Remove the skins and cut into fine slivers.

Finely chop the orange peel and mixed peel. Mix almonds, orange peel, mixed peel and rasins with the rum, cover with cling-film and leave at room temperature.

DAY 2

STARTER
Weigh the flour and sugar in a bowl. Dissolve the yeast in the milk and pour over the flour. Knead for 10 minutes on the lowest speed until elastic. Place the dough in a lightly oiled plastic container with a lid and leave to rise for 30 minutes in a warm place until doubled in size.

KNEADING
1. Cut the vanilla pod into small pieces and weigh the spices. Scald the almonds and bitter almond in boiling water and rinse under cold water. Remove the skins and mix the almonds, vanilla, spices, grated lemon rind and 20 g of sugar until smooth.
2. Weigh the flour and add the starter together with the egg yolk, sugar and salt. Knead for 2 minutes on the lowest speed and add the soft butter, a little at a time. Knead for approx. 15 minutes until elastic. Test the dough for elasticity.
3. Mix in the marinated fruit. If you knead for too long, the dough will get brown and sticky. Place the dough in a lightly oiled lidded plastic container and leave for 30 minutes in the unheated oven. Knock back and leave for another 20 minutes.
4. Turn out on a floured work surface and divide in two. Make two taut, round balls, cover with a tea-towel and leave for 10 minutes.
5. Make two oblong loaves. Make two strips of almond paste, slightly shorter than the bread.
6. Roll out the dough in the middle, so the edges get thicker. Place a roll of almond paste in the middle, fold over the dough and press with the rolling pin.
7. Move to a tray with a baking sheet and leave to rise until almost doubled in size in the unheated oven, approx. 45–60 minutes. Spray with water a couple of times to avoid the surface from drying out. Remove the bread.
8. Preheat the oven to 230°C. Place the tray in the warm oven and spray generously with water.
9. Lower the temperature to 180°C after 5 minutes. Bake for 40 minutes until golden brown. Use a thermometer to check that they are ready (98°C).
10. Take out the tray and leave to cool for 30 minutes.
11. Glace both sides with butter until most has been absorbed.
12. Turn over in castor sugar and leave to cool.
13. Sift over vanilla-flavoured sugar and place in plastic bags.

Tip
The stollen keeps for several weeks. It matures and often tastes better after a while. Enjoy thin slices with coffee or a glass of sweet, German wine.

Decorative Bread

It is not as hard to make decorative bread as you might think. This dough is suitable for rustic decorative bread, an excellent gift, or for harvest bread.

500 g water (5 dl)	150 g wholemeal flour,
30 g yeast	preferably stone ground
500 g fine rye flour,	200 g strong wheat flour
preferably stone ground	30 g butter
200 g coarse rye flour,	20 g sea salt
preferably stone ground	

1. Place all the ingredients in a bowl except butter and salt.
2. Knead for 20 minutes until elastic. Add salt and butter after 10 minutes.
3. Place the dough in a lightly oiled plastic container with a lid and leave for 60 minutes.
4. Turn out on a work top dusted with flour and cut off a 200 g piece. (The dough should be dense.)
5. Make a ball from the remaining dough. Shape a round, 4 cm, thick base using a rolling pin. Brush with water.
6. Roll out a string from 150 g of dough, divide into 15 pieces and make round balls. Arrange in the form of a bunch of grapes (see pic. p. 221). Roll out the remaining dough and cut out a vine leaf. Make the pattern with the back of a knife.
7. Spray with water and add the leaf. Roll out a couple of strings of the remaining dough and place on the bread. Sift over fine rye flour. Trim the edge with a pair of scissors. Place on a baking tray.
8. Cover with a tea towel and leave to rise for approx. 45 minutes until it has increased in size by 50%.
9. Preheat the oven to 250ºC.
10. Put the tray in the oven and spray generously with water.
11. Lower the temperature to 200ºC after 5 minutes. Open the oven door after another 10 minutes to let some air in.
12. Bake for a total of 60 minutes.
13. Remove and cool on the tray.

Ornamental Bread

This type of bread is mainly for decoration. Craft shops sell templates.

Off-white dough

900 g strong wheat flour	20 g sea salt
100 g fine rye flour	500 g water (5 dl)
50 g butter	

White dough

1,000 g strong wheat flour,	40 g sea salt
preferably stone ground	400 g water (4 dl)
200 g butter	

Knead all the ingredients for 20 minutes on the lowest speed, increase the speed towards the end. Keep in an airtight plastic container in the fridge.

Boiled dough for decoration

1,000 g fine rye flour,	350 g water (3.5 dl)
preferably stone ground	350 g sugar

Put the flour in a bowl. Bring water and sugar to the boil, immediately pour over the flour and mix until smooth. Transfer to a lightly oiled plastic container with a lid and leave overnight.

Salt dough

800 g strong wheat flour	1,000 g table salt
200 g fine rye flour,	500 g water (5 dl)
preferably stone ground	500 g vatten (5 dl)

Mix for 10 minutes on low speed. Keep in a plastic container with a lid in the fridge.

Christmas motif (see p. 213)

1. Make a round base from 1,000 g white dough. Clip around the edge with a pair of scissors.
2. Make a batch of icing, see p. 223. Draw a deer on a sheet of overhead film and cut out. Place the template on the dough, apply a thin layer of icing and remove the template.
3. Roll out a thin piece of decoration dough and cut out a strip of dough. Write "Merry Christmas" using a small paper cone and the icing.
4. Bake for 60 minutes at 175ºC.

Make Easter bread in the same way, just change the caption.

Decorative Shellfish Bread

Use one of the doughs on p. 218. Make a round base and
mould various marine creatures from the pliant dough.
Spray with water. Sift some chilli powder over the crab,
curry and tumeric over the others and a little cocoa powder.
(Picture p. 94).

Decorative Bread with Hare and Wheatears

Use one of the doughs on p. 218. Make an oval base and
cut around the edges with a pair of scissors. Make dough
wheatears (see p. 219) and spray with water. Sift over
turmeric. Make the hare and paint with cocoa powder and
water. Bake as for Christmas Motif on p. 218.

Decorative Vegetable Bread
Use decorative dough, see p. 218. Make a round base and shape vegetables, see p. 107. I dipped the potato in cocoa powder and decorated with herbs and tomato puré. Follow the baking instructions on p. 218.

Decorative Bread with Grapes
Use decorative dough, see p. 218. Make a round base and cut the edge with a pair of scissors. Place a plate in the centre and glaze with water around the edges. Sift over a little fine rye flour. Make dough grapes and arrange. Glaze with beaten egg. Roll out the dough and cut out vine leaves, score with the back of a knife and glaze with egg. Make tendrils and glaze with egg. Follow baking instructions on p. 218. (Picture p. 166).

Decorative Bread with Lady Motif
Use decorative dough, see p. 218. Make a round base and cut the edge with a pair of scissors. Place a plate in the centre and glaze with water around the edges. Sift over a little fine rye flour. Remove the plate and shape the motif. Glaze with egg. Follow baking instructions on p. 218. (Picture p. 166).

Decorative Wedding Bread
This is a nice gift to bring to a wedding party. The bread featured on p. 216 is made from Zopf dough. See p. 65.

1. Place the dough on a floured work surface and cut off a 400 g piece of dough.
2. Make a ball from the larger piece, place it on a baking tray and press to make a round loaf. Spray with water and sift over a layer of cocoa power using a tea strainer.
3. Divide the remaining dough into four pieces.
4. Make two bread doves, brush the back with water and attach to the loaf. Roll out the rest of the dough and place around the edges.

5. Leave for 30 minutes. Bake for 60 minutes at 175ºC.
6. Cool on a wire rack.

Flower Pot Bread
This is a nice gift to bring to a party. (Picture p. 216). Use the same dough as for Decorative Bread, p. 218, and follow the instructions for preparing the dough.

1. Soak a terracotta flower pot in cold water for 30 minutes.
2. Make a dough ball that fills half the pot. Grease the inside walls of the pot with soft butter and put a piece of baking paper on the bottom to prevent the dough from sticking.
3. Make a bread flower and sprinkle with any kind of seeds after brushing with water. Leave to rise until it reaches the top of the pot, glaze with beaten egg.
4. Preheat the oven to 175ºC. Bake the pot and flower for approx. 45 minutes.
5. Take out the bread and leave to cool. Add potato flour to a teaspoon of water and use to attach the flower.

Icing for writing on bread
Use this for piping or using with templates before baking.

50 g wheat flour	12 g cocoa powder
25 g icing sugar	45 g water (0.45 dl)

Sift wheat flour, icing sugar and cocoa onto a piece of paper and pour into a small bowl. Add the water and stir to make a light batter.

What to do with leftover bread

Breadcrumbs used with meat or fish is the traditional use for leftover bread, but it is now less common.

- Soak leftover bread in milk and mix with mince meat for a lighter mince.

- Grate yesterday's bread and use as breadcrumbs or mix with mince meat.

- Slice stale baguette thinly, brush with flavoured olive oil and toast in the oven. These *crostini* go well with soup, or serve as a cocktail snack with a suitable topping.

- Make croutons for soups and salads. Dice the bread, rub a frying pan with garlic and fry in a mixture of butter and olive oil.

- Farmer's loaf can be sliced, lightly rubbed with a garlic clove and fried in a little olive oil. A leaner alternative is to toast the slices in the oven. Use for making bruschetta.

- Fried bread: Remove the crusts from toasting bread and fry in a mixture of oil and butter. Drain on a baking sheet and serve fresh.

- Toast Melba: Remove the crusts from a white loaf, slice thinly and toast in a medium oven.

- Canapés are thin slices of buttered sandwich bread or bread slices fried in butter with a fancy topping, e.g. caviare.

- Two classics are Bread Pudding and Summer Pudding.

- A specialty from Skåne is *ölsupa* (bread soup) and apple crumble made with leftover bread.

- Dip slices of white loaf in pancake batter, fry and sprinkle with cinnamon and sugar.

Bread and Butter Pudding

This winter dessert was always popular with our British and American passengers when I used to work on cruise liners. Serve warm with warm vanilla custard.

6 servings
An oval, oven-proof dish, 24 cm long and 2 cm deep

VANILLA CUSTARD	250 g full-fat milk (2.5 dl)
1/2 vanilla pod, preferably from Tahiti	60 g egg yolk (3)
	50 g sugar

1. Divide the vanilla pod lengthwise and store the remaining half in an air tight container.
2. Pour the milk and vanilla in a small saucepan and bring to the boil, giving it an occasional stir. Set to the side to infuse.
3. Whisk egg yolks and sugar and pour over the milk, mix carefully. Put the saucepan back on the heat and stir until the custard starts to thicken. Dip the spoon in the custard and blow on it. It should crease when it is ready. Use a thermometer to check the temperature, 85°C, the custard will separate if it gets too hot.
4. Pour through a strainer and cover immediately with cling-film.

70 California raisins	a pinch of sea salt
200 g butter	1/2 a vanilla pod,
10 slices of toasting bread, see p. 53	preferably from Tahiti
	250 g egg (5 eggs)
300 g full-fat milk (3 dl)	60 g sugar
300 g double cream (3 dl)	25 g butter for greasing

1. Put the raisins in plenty of cold water and soak for 30 minutes. Drain. Melt the butter in a small saucepan. Remove the crusts from the bread and cut into triangles, dip in the butter and place in the dish. Sprinkle with raisins.
2. Bring milk, cream, salt and the vanilla to the boil. Leave to infuse.
3. Whisk egg and sugar briefly and pour over the milk. Strain over the dish.
4. Preheat the oven to 150°C.
5. Place the dish in a roasting tin and pour 1 l of boiling water around it. Bake for approx. 60 minutes until golden. Serve with warm custard.

Apple Cake from Skåne

This is a very typical regional dish. The rye bread in the breadcrumbs is very important.

8–10 servings
22 cm spring mould

250 g grated dark rye bread	350 g sugar
250 g bread crumbs	50 g butter
250 g butter	
1 tbsp cinnamon	breadcrumbs and butter.
1,000 g apple sections, preferably Cox's Orange	
75 g lemon juice (0.75 dl)	

1. Grate the same amount of dark rye bread as there are breadcrumbs.
2. Brown 250 g of butter.
3. Add the breadcrumbs (500 g) and 1 tbsp freshly ground cinnamon. Toast the bread while stirring.
4. Boil 1,000 g apple sections, 75 g lemon juice, 350 g sugar and 50 g butter on high heat until the mixture no longer sticks to the saucepan.
5. Layer breadcrumbs and apple sauce in a round mould. Top with breadcrumbs and butter. Bake at 200°C for 30 minutes and serve warm with vanilla custard.

Soft Apple Cake

Use crushed rusks for the mould. I learned to make this delicious, simple and very popular cake at age 16, when I was working at a patisserie in Malmö. We made 24 at the time, every other day.

1 cake
1 round 1.5 l tin

300 g apples (preferably Cox's Orange)	100 g egg (2 eggs)
5 g cinnamon	200 g milk (2 dl)
10 g sugar	300 g wheat flour
	12 g baking powder
160 g butter	25 g rusk crumbs for the mould
340 g sugar	
grated rind of 1 lemon	25 g butter for the mould

Continued on p. 229

Bread and Butter Pudding together with Apple Cake from Skåne.

Cherry Pudding and Soft Apple Cake (p. 226).

1. Peel 300 g of apples, remove the pips, cut into sections and mix with cinnamon and sugar.
2. Mix the soft butter and sugar until light and fluffy.
3. Grate the washed lemon and add to the butter.
4. Add the eggs, one at the time, while stirring.
5. Add the milk, sift over the flour and baking powder and stir until smooth.
6. Preheat the oven to 175°C.
7. Butter the tin and sprinkle generously with crushed rusk.
8. Pour in the batter and put the apple sections over the top.
9. Bake for 45–50 minutes, use a baking needle to check if it is ready. Remove from the tin.
10. Cool on a wire rack.

Serve cold with coffee or warm with vanilla ice cream.

Cherry Pudding

At the Honold Confiserie in Zürich, we used to make cherry pudding every day. We soaked leftover toasting bread in milk in the afternoon and and left it overnight. We greased the tins with butter and mixed rusk crumbs with 1 part sandel flour and 9 parts rusk crumbs. We poured the mixture into the fluted tins and discarded the surplus. This mixture gave the puddings a nice colour in the oven. Serve warm with whipped cream spiked with Kirschwasser or with vanilla custard.

Use tinned cherries sold in Asian shops. If you are lucky enough to have a cherry tree in your garden, just remove the stones and they are ready to use.

6–8 servings
1 fluted 2 l tin

DAY 1
160 g white bread, no crusts
200 g milk (2 dl)

DAY 2
100 g almonds
5 g bitter almonds
1 lemon
600 g black cherries, e.g. stoned morellos

100 g butter
100 g sugar
5 g freshly grated real cinnamon
80 g egg yolk (4)
1 tsp lemon juice
25 g sugar
15 g potato flour

FOR THE TIN
25 g butter
45 g rusk crumbs
5 g sandel flour, available from herb shops, delis

DAY 1
Soak the bread in milk over night.

DAY 2
1. Bring the water to the boil and scald the bitter almonds and almonds together. Rinse under cold running water. Remove the skins and dry on a towel.
2. Preheat the oven to 100°C, place the almonds on the open oven door and dry for 30 minutes. Grind.
3. Wash the lemons and grate half, or the flavour will get overpowering.
4. Drain the stoned cherries in a colander.
5. Brush the inside of the tin with the soft butter. Sprinkle with the crumb mixture and shake out the surplus.
6. Pour the soaked bread into a mixer and mix until smooth.
7. Place the soft butter in a bowl and add 100 g sugar, cinnamon and lemon rind. Use an electric whisk to beat the butter light and creamy.
8. Add the egg yolks one at a time, whisk until smooth.
9. Fold in the bread mixture and mix until smooth.
10. Rub the inside of a metal or copper bowl with white vinegar and salt to remove any fatty residues. Rinse in cold water.
11. Add the egg white, lemon juice and 25 g sugar and whisk on medium speed until firm. Stop the mixer, sift in potato flour and whisk for another minute.
12. Fold in the whisked egg and then the cherries.
13. Preheat the oven to 170°C.
14. Pour the batter into the tin and place in the oven. Bake for approx. 45 minutes until firm and dry at the centre. Check with a thermometer. The temperature should be 98°C.
15. Remove the tin from the oven and leave for 10 minutes. Remove the tin and place on a pretty plate. Serve warm with lightly whipped cream with a little sugar and a drop of Kirschwasser or some other spirit, brandy for example.

Conversion Table

WEIGHT		VOLUME		WEIGHT		VOLUME	
Metric (g/kg)	Imperial (oz/lb)	Metric (ml/l)	Imperial (oz/pints)	Metric (g/kg)	Imperial (oz/lb)	Metric (ml/l)	Imperial (oz/pints)
		1.25 ml	¼ teaspoon	350 g	12 oz	1.2 litre	2 pints
10 g	¼ oz	2.5 ml	½ teaspoon	375 g	13 oz	1.3 litre	2 ¼ pints
15 g	½ oz	5 ml	1 teaspoon	400 g	14 oz	1.4 litre	2 ½ pints
25-30 g	1 oz	10 ml	2 teaspoon	425 g	15 oz	1.5 litre	2 ¾ pints
35 g	1 ¼ oz	15 ml	½ fl oz	450 g	1 lb	1.7 litre	3 pints
40 g	1 ½ oz	30 ml	1 fl oz	500 g	1 lb 2 oz		
50 g	1 ¾ oz	50 ml	2 fl oz	550 g	1 lb 4 oz		
55 g	2 oz	75 ml	2 ½ fl oz	600 g	1 lb 5 oz		
60 g	2 ¼ oz	100 ml	3 ½ fl oz	650 g	1 lb 7 oz		
70 g	2 ½ oz	125 ml	4 fl oz	700 g	1 lb 9 oz		
85 g	3 oz	150 ml	5 fl oz ¼ pint	750 g	1 lb 10 oz		
90 g	3 ¼ oz	175 ml	6 fl oz	800 g	1 lb 12 oz		
100 g	3 ½ oz	200 ml	7 fl oz	850 g	1 lb 14 oz		
115 g	4 oz	225 ml	8 fl oz	900 g	2 lb		
125 g	4 ½ oz	250 ml	9 fl oz	950 g	2 lb 2 oz		
140 g	5 oz	300 ml	10 fl oz ½ pint	1 kg	2 lb 4 oz		
150 g	5 ½ oz	350 ml	12 fl oz	1.25 kg	2 lb 12 oz		
175 g	6 oz	400 ml	14 fl oz	1.3 kg	3 lb		
200 g	7 oz	425 ml	15 fl oz ¾ pint	1.5 kg	3 lb 5 oz		
225 g	8 oz	450 ml	16 fl oz	1.6 kg	3 lb 8 oz		
250 g	9 oz	500 ml	18 fl oz	1.8 kg	4 lb		
275 g	9 ¼ oz	600 ml	20 fl oz 1 pint	2 kg	4 lb 8 oz		
280 g	10 oz	700 ml	1 ¼ pint	2.25 kg	5 lb		
300 g	10 ½ oz	850 ml	1 ½ pint	2.5 kg	5 lb 8 oz		
325 g	11 ½ oz	1 litre	1 ¾ pint	2.7 kg	6 lb		
				3 kg	6 lb 8 oz		

ARTISAN BREAD.